"Bring the Classics to Life"

ROBINSON CRUSOE

LEVEL 3

Series Designer
Philip J. Solimene

Editor
Virginia B. Heflin

EDCON

Story Adaptor

Virginia B. Heflin

Author

Daniel Defoe

Original story published in England in 1719, based upon a real happening in the life of Alexander Selkirk, 1704 to 1709.

Copyright © 1995

A/V Concepts Corp.

30 Montauk Blvd., Oakdale, NY 11769

info@edconpublishing.com

Visit our Web site at: www.edconpublishing.com

Printed in U.S.A.
ISBN 0-931334-30-6

CONTENTS

NO.	TITLE	SYNOPSIS	PAGE
1	I Long for the Sea	Against his father's wishes and even though his first trip ended in ship wreck, Robinson Crusoe chooses the life of the sea. It was 1651 and he was 19 years old.	6
2	Eight Years Later — and Ship Wrecked!	Robinson Crusoe had done so well on his first trading trip to Africa that he was now going again, even though he had been taken over by pirates on one such trip. Only twelve days out from his plantation in Brazil he was ship wrecked and alone.	12
3	Settling In	Robinson Crusoe built himself a fortress on his island, using many things from the wrecked ship. He made tables, chairs, and baskets; grew corn for seed; hunted birds and goats; and found turtle eggs.	18
4	I Find Peace — and Grow to be Happy	Being very sick and having a troubling dream led Robinson Crusoe to find peace through reading his Bible and thanking God for all his good. After that, he worked to make his island life pleasant and happy.	24
5	I Truly Work for my Bread	To get bread Robinson Crusoe dug up the ground, planted seed, and guarded the plants from the birds. Then he made earthen jars for storing grain. Out of a tree trunk he made a mortar and pestle for grinding the rice and barley. He used a neck scarf for a sieve to sift the flour. Then he made an earthen oven for baking the bread.	30
6	Quiet Happenings — and Frightening!	Robinson Crusoe made clothes and an umbrella from animal skins. He made a boat from a tree trunk and was almost lost at sea. After 15 years of peace and safety, he saw a frightening foot print.	36
7	Cannibals on my Island!	Robinson Crusoe made his fortress stronger and found a large cave in which he stored his gun powder. Once he saw bones of people on the shore and later, after 22 years on his island, he saw the cannibals actually holding their terrible feast.	42
8	My Man, Friday!	In 1684, after 25 years alone, Robinson Crusoe saved from the cannibals a man he named Friday, who served him faithfully the rest of his life.	48
9	We Win — and Get a Happy Surprise!	Friday told Robinson Crusoe of white men living on the mainland with his people, and they built a boat to go there. Cannibals came to the island to feast on four men. When Robinson Crusoe saw that one was not a cannibal, they went to save him. Then another of the prisoners turned out to be Friday's own father!	54
10	Back to England!	In 1686 an English ship stopped near the island because the sailors had turned against the Captain. After Robinson Crusoe and Friday helped get his ship back, the Captain put himself under Robinson Crusoe's order. So he went back to England in style.	60

WORDS USED

Story 1	Story 2	Story 3	Story 4	Story 5
KEY WORDS				
bend	blanket	class	desk	bench
bundle	chatter	crack	hall	chance
gather	crept	finally	jar	coach
root	curtain	hang	job	lose
snapped	enjoy	replied	sidewalk	team
son	freeze	thirty	special	worry
SPECIAL WORDS				
England	Africa	calendar	deliver	barley
London	Brazil	fortress	guilt	bran
York	captain	mast	parrot	bushel
	Orinoco	oar	prayer	earth
	pirate	powder	raisins	rice
	plantation	raft	tobacco	scarf
NECESSARY WORDS				
gun	cabin	against	also	broke
longing	English	barrel	Bible	dried
mainly	learn	cave	die	earthen
September	north	chain	dream	flat
ship	pound	God	dry	grown
sick	sail	island	fast	hour
	sugar	meat	forgive	month
	teeth	mile	grape	Poll
	trade	post	hid	pot
	wreck	rat	mind	raked
		settle	peace	shake
		Sunday	rum	shaped
		tide	season	shot
		tool	weak	thin

WORDS USED

Story 6	Story 7	Story 8	Story 9	Story 10
KEY WORDS				
chew	fur	already	autumn	awake
dash	mile	boots	danger	forget
meant	moment	cave	excitement	forgot
meat	rule	eager	gun	lose
rid	rush	matter	less	promise
spoil	sidewalk	pack	shot	twenty
SPECIAL WORDS				
comfortably	cannibal	Caribs	chopped	drunk
current	disgust	Christian	pray	fought
herd	feast	master	puzzled	Governor
loose	flesh	sword	rudder	keep sake
umbrella	scattered	tribe	Spaniard	nephew
valuable	telescope	Trinidad	yelling	worst
NECESSARY WORDS				
cheese	added	Friday	ax	December
fan	blood	grind	bloody	hang
ink	built	save	clear	law
joy	dead	spoke	clearly	leader
main	dripping	sweetest	mad	married
pants	fear	understand	mainland	order
pen	hidden	war	tear	sailor
pit	mine		untie	shooting
sand	shore			welcome
sight	upon			whole
skin				women
smoke				yard arm
vegetable				

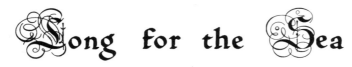

I Long for the Sea

PREPARATION

Key Words

bend	(bend)	to push or pull something until it looks different; not straight *A strong wind came along and made the straight little tree bend way over.* to reach down *Bend over and pick up the pretty stones.* to give in to someone or something *I will bend to your will; I will do what you want me to do.*
bundle	(bun′ dl)	a number of things that are put together and kept together in some way *Mrs. Stone gathered the dirty clothes into a bundle before she washed them.* to tie several things together into a ball or roll *We bundled our things into a back pack to go camping.*
gather	(gaᴛʜ′ ər)	to bring a number of things into one place *Chipmunks gather nuts and put them in holes in trees.* to come together *Everyone gather around and let's talk about it.* gather up, to pick up and put together *Gather up the dirty dishes to wash them.*
root	(rüt)	part of a plant that grows under the ground *A tree will die when its roots do not get enough water.* the under or bottom part, not seen, from which something grows or happens *My longing to be free from my father was at the root of my leaving home.*
snapped	(snapt)	to have broken quickly with a sudden sound *As Mary started to climb the tree, the branch snapped and broke in her hand.* closed with a quick, little noise *I snapped my hand bag shut.* made a quick bite *The dog snapped at the mail carrier.*
son	(sun)	male child of a father and mother *The elephant's son looks just like his father, but is much smaller.* one belonging to something larger and older, as a country or idea *We are all sons of our world.*

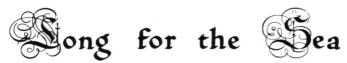 # I Long for the Sea

Special Words

England   (ing′ glənd)   a country, a very large island near Europe
The grandmothers and grandfathers of many people in America came from England.

London   (lun′ dən)   the most important city in England, its capital
London is an old and important city.

York   (yôrk)   a city in north east England
The city of New York was named after York, England.

Necessary Words

gun   (gun)   a long pipe made for shooting, used mostly for killing
People use guns in fighting and hunting.
something that looks like or works like a gun
We used a spray gun to paint the bicycle.
to start very fast
The driver gunned the car.

longing   (lông′ ing)   a deep wanting that lasts a long time
I had a longing to go visit my old home again.

mainly   (mān′ lē)   mostly; for the most part; largely
The main idea of the story is what it is mainly about.

September   (sep tem′ bər)   the month that is number nine in the year
Fall begins in September.

ship   (ship)   something like a boat but much bigger, used for long trips over water
Ships can carry many large things as well as people.
something large for carrying people or things that sails in water or air
Airplanes are sometimes called air ships.
to send something by ship, train, truck, or airplane
We shipped the box last Monday.

sick   (sik)   not well
A cold can make you feel sick.
throwing up one's food
the moving waves of the sea made me sea sick.

I Long for the Sea

Robinson Crusoe left his home in York, England, and went to Hull. There he went on board a ship which was later wrecked near Yarmouth. He walked on to London to find another ship.

Preview:
1. Read the name of the story.
2. Look at the picture carefully.
3. Read the sentences under the picture.
4. Read the first two paragraphs of the story.
5. Then, answer the following question.

You learned from your preview that Robinson Crusoe had wanted to go to sea

_____ a. for a year.

_____ b. for many years.

_____ c. all his life.

_____ d. for a few years.

Turn to the Comprehension Check on page 10 for the right answer.

Now read the story.

Read to find out how much Robinson Crusoe wanted to go to sea.

I Long for the Sea

I was almost 19 when I set foot on that first ship. It was on September 1, 1651. I had walked two days from my home in York, England, down to the sea. Now I was off to London on my first sea trip.

All my life I had had deep inside me this great longing to go to sea. It was like a great tree root growing deep within me, getting bigger and bigger.

My father and mother wanted me to stay home. I was their last son. One had been killed fighting for England. As for the other son, no one knew what had happened to him.

A year ago, my father had talked to me. He would do well by me. There was the big farm and lots of money for me. Crying, my father had said, "If you go to sea, you will live to be sad about it."

I really tried to stay home. But the pull of the sea was too strong.

Down at the sea, I had met a friend who took me to his father's ship. He told me to gather up my things and just come on board.

A short trip to London would let me find out for sure if I really wanted the life of the sea. Quickly, I put my bundle of clothes on board ship.

The first day at sea turned out to be a bad start. Almost at once, a strong wind blew up. It made our ship bend over and back up, again and again. I got very sea sick. I was so frightened that I told myself I would surely go back home. My father was right.

But two days later, I was feeling fit and fine again. The wind was quiet. The tiny waves danced in the sun. The sea was the most beautiful thing I had ever seen. By the end of five days, the call of the sea was as strong as ever.

Then came a wind blowing so hard the wrong way that we could not go the way we wanted. After eight days, the wind turned into a terrible storm. Our ship rolled and rocked. Water came in faster than we could get it out. Everyone was frightened. There was nothing to do but leave the ship. The owner fired the guns for help and shouted, "Everyone gather on top!" At last, a small boat came and took us off. With the wind and the waves high around us, we looked back at our ship. It had snapped into pieces! In just 15 minutes it went down into the stormy sea!

Rowing very hard, we got to land at last. We reached and took hold of some little tree roots sticking out and pulled our little boat up close. If they had snapped off, we would have fallen into the water. But we were lucky.

The people in the town gave us food, clothes, and money. They took us into their homes. How glad we were to be safe!

Two days later, out walking, I saw my friend again. That was when he told his father that I had gone on this trip just to find out if I liked seagoing.

On hearing this, his father said to me, "Young man, you should never go to sea again! Take this as a sign to you."

Then the owner thought about his ship down at the bottom of the sea. "Why," he said, "maybe we lost our ship because of you. Never again will I set foot on the same ship with you!"

When next I saw him, the owner was more kindly. But still he said, "Young man, DO NOT go to sea. If you do, only bad things will happen to you. Many times you will think of your father's words."

But again, I would not listen to my head. Why? I really can't say. My will just would not bend. Picking up my bundle of clothes, off I went, walking to London.

I Long for the Sea

COMPREHENSION CHECK

Choose the best answer.

1. His longing to go to sea was
    ___ a. like going on a long trip.
    ___ b. a great, growing tree root.
    ___ c. something he sometimes wanted.
    ___ d. a deep wanting that grew and grew.

2. His father wanted him to
    ___ a. go to sea.
    ___ b. buy a big farm.
    ___ c. fight for England.
    ___ d. stay at home.

3. He tried to stay at home because
    ___ a. his friend's father told him not to go to sea.
    ___ b. the ship's owner would not go on board ship with him again.
    ___ c. he was needed at home to fight for England.
    ___ d. his father and mother would be sad if he went to sea.

4. The first day at sea,
    ___ a. the wind blew very hard.
    ___ b. the sea was beautiful.
    ___ c. there was a terrible storm.
    ___ d. the ship went down.

5. After eight days of the storm,
    ___ a. they got to London.
    ___ b. the wind was quiet.
    ___ c. everyone was sea sick.
    ___ d. they left the ship.

6. They were lucky when they got to land because
    ___ a. they rowed very hard.
    ___ b. they could pull the boat up close.
    ___ c. the tree roots snapped off.
    ___ d. the boat did not turn over.

7. His friend's father said that the ship going down was
    ___ a. a bad start for him.
    ___ b. what his father said would happen.
    ___ c. a sign to him not to go to sea again.
    ___ d. what happens on most sea trips.

8. At the end of the story, he
    ___ a. is going back to sea.
    ___ b. gives up a life on the sea.
    ___ c. goes to live with his mother and father.
    ___ d. goes to live in London.

9. Another name for the story could be
    ___ a. "A Storm at Sea."
    ___ b. "Do as Your Father Tells You To Do."
    ___ c. "A Trip to London."
    ___ d. "A Bad Start, But Not an End."

10. This story is mainly about
    ___ a. life at sea.
    ___ b. a young man's first sea trip.
    ___ c. a ship going down at sea.
    ___ d. leaving home for the first time.

Check your answers with the key on page 67.

ong for the ea

VOCABULARY CHECK

bundle	roots	snapped	gather	bend	son

I. Sentences to Finish

Using the words in the big box above, choose the one which best fits in each of the sentences below. Write the words on the lines in the sentences.

1. The boys tied all the papers together into one big _____ .

2. The man is so strong that he can _____ a horseshoe until it is straight.

3. To remember to take with you all the things you want, _____ them all together in one place.

4. The _____ of plants are as large as the part above the **ground**.

5. The father was very proud of his _____ because the boy looked so much like him.

6. When his mother came in, the boy quickly _____ the box shut because it held a surprise for her birthday.

II. Crossword Puzzle

Fill in the little boxes with the letters of the words at the top of the page. The numbers in the puzzle match the numbers of the sentences below. The sentences will help you guess which word fits each set of boxes.

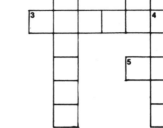

Across

1. You do this when you pick up something from the floor.

3. Water will _____ in low places.

5. A boy is a _____ to his father.

Down

1. You put things into a _____ to make them easier to carry.

2. In the storm the tree branch _____ off and fell to the ground.

4. All plants have these.

Check your answers with the key on page 69.

Eight Years Later—and Ship Wrecked!

PREPARATION

Key Words

blanket	(blang' kit)	something that covers *He used a blanket to keep him warm.* to blanket *The snow blanketed the ground.*
chatter	(chat' ər)	talk in a quick, silly way *We could hear the monkey chatter in his cage.* to talk lots and fast about things that are not important *The happy people chattered about many things at the picnic.* to make quick sounds by knocking things together many times *Our teeth chatter when we are very cold.* quick, not clear sounds *The chatter of the birds could be heard every morning.*
crept	(krept)	moved in a slow way, crawled on floor or ground *The baby crept to his mother.* came quietly, slowly, little by little *The river crept higher and higher until it went over its banks.* grew little by little *The plants crept along the wall.*
curtain	(kėrt' n)	a cover on the glass of a window or a door *The curtains are in the window.* a large cloth covering the inside of the glass of a window *The people inside the house can look out through the curtain, but those on the outside cannot see in.* thing that covers or hides *The fog made such a curtain around us that we could not see across the street.*
enjoy	(en joi')	be happy with *We will enjoy playing with the new toys.* have as a good thing *I enjoy a nice home.* have a good time *I enjoyed going to the show.*
freeze	(frēz)	to turn to ice *The water began to freeze when it got very cold.* to turn hard *You have to freeze milk and other things to make ice cream.* to get very cold because of being frightened *That sound is so terrible it makes me freeze.*

Eight Years Later—and ShipWrecked!

Special Words

Africa (af′ rə kə) the continent south of Europe, the second largest continent
Africa is a beautiful place with many wild animals.

Brazil (brə zil′) a large country in South America
Much of our coffee comes from Brazil.

captain (kap′ tən) the head one of a group, the leader
I was basketball captain in my last year of school.
the one in charge of a ship
The captain watches over the running of the ship.

Orinoco (or′ ə nō′ kō) a large river in South America flowing easterly through Venezuela into the North Atlantic Ocean
The island of Trinidad is near the northern part of the mouth of the Orinoco River.

pirate (pī′ rit) robber on the sea, man who robs ships
The pirates used fast ships to catch other ships.

plantation (plan tā′ shən) a large farm, nearly always in a hot or warm part of the world, on which is grown cotton, sugar cane, or rubber trees
The plantation was so large that it had over 100 workers.

Necessary Words

cabin (kab′ ən) a small house
We went to our cabin in the woods.
a small room on a boat
Each one on the ship had a cabin with a bed and a place to keep clothes.

English (ing′ glish) of or having to do with England, its people or their way of talking
English dishes are very fine.

learn (lėrn) find out how to do something through study, class, or by doing it over and over
I learned how to drive a car.

north (nôrth) the way to your right as you face the sun when it sets
As the sun went down, I looked at it and pointed my right arm straight out to the north.
the northern part of any country
The North had a cold winter.

pound (pound) a measure of weight; 16 ounces
I bought a pound of coffee.
English money made of silver
An English pound was worth about 7½ dollars ($7.50) in Robinson Crusoe's time.

sail (sāl) a piece of cloth tied to a mast with ropes
The wind blew into the sail and carried the boat over the water.
to go on a trip on a boat or ship
I love to go sailing.

sugar (shu̇g′ ər) sweet crystals usually made from sugar beets or sugar cane
The juice squeezed from sugar cane is boiled down to make sugar.

teeth (tēth) rows of hard bone-like parts of the mouth used for biting and chewing
I brush my teeth morning and night to keep them clean and white.

trade (trād) to buy and sell
I traded my old car for a better one.
having to do with buying and selling
Many trade ships went from country to country.

wreck (rek) what is left of something that has been torn up
The car was such a wreck that I don't know how anyone got out alive.

Eight Years Later—and ShipWrecked!

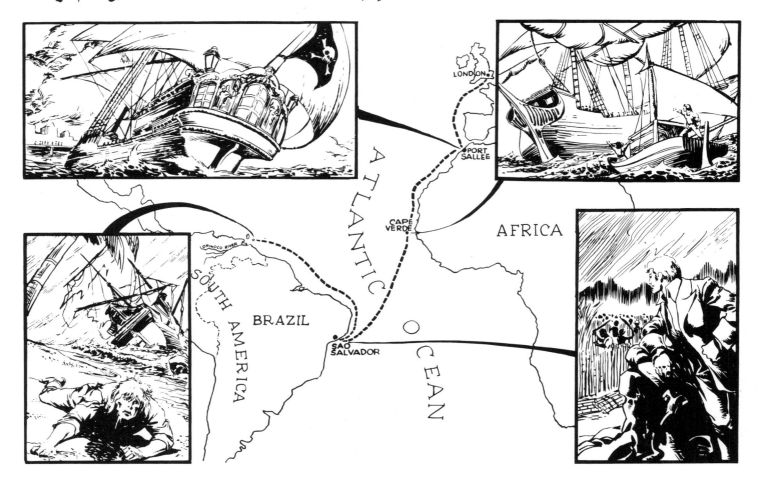

From London, Robinson Crusoe went on trading trips to Africa. On his second trip, pirates captured him and took him to Port Sallee'. After more than two years, he escaped in a long boat and was picked up by a ship going to Brazil.

In Brazil, he became a plantation owner and was growing rich. He and his friends needed workers for their plantation. So, he set out to sail to Africa and trade for them. On the way, he was shipwrecked in the mouth of the Orinoco River, not far from Trinidad Island.

Preview: 1.   Read the name of the story.
2.   Look at the picture carefully.
3.   Read the sentences under the picture.
4.   Read the first paragraph of the story.
5.   Then, answer the following question.

You learned from your preview that
_____ a.   something will happen to change his life.
_____ b.   he will have a life on the sea.
_____ c.   he will be captain of a ship.
_____ d.   the ship he is on will be wrecked.

Turn to the Comprehension Check on page 16 for the right answer.

Now read the story.

Read to find out what happened in the eight years since Robinson Crusoe left home.

Eight Years Later – and ShipWrecked!

Just eight years after I first set foot on a ship, I set sail on the most important trip of my life. On September 1, 1659, I sailed from Brazil, going to Africa. There I would enjoy trading with the people and would bring back workers for our sugar plantations.

How did I get to Brazil? And why was I the one to go to do this trading?

Back in London, I had met an English captain who took me on his ship to Africa. He showed me how to sail a ship and how to trade with the people. I had turned 40 pounds ($100) into 300 pounds ($750). That was my best trip.

My second trip to Africa was very different. On our way down, pirates took us over. The pirate captain kept me for his own.

What a terrible life! For longer than two years I had no hope of getting away. The only good thing was that I did not freeze as I had in England. North Africa is warm.

Then, one day, I was sent out fishing in the longboat. It had a cabin on it in which were tables, beds, and blankets. There were even curtains at the cabin windows! This lucky day there was much food and some guns on board. When I got out to sea, I just kept sailing.

I followed along the land of Africa for 28 days before seeing a large ship. I fired off a gun for help.

The ship was going to Brazil.

The good captain took me on board. He bought the longboat and everything I had on it.

I went on land in Brazil with 220 pieces of gold. In the next four years, I did very well. I was on the road to being able to enjoy great money. But always, the thought crept up on me, "I could have done this back in England on my father's farm."

Many times I remembered my trips to Africa. Sometimes I would chatter about how easy it was to trade toys, bits of glass, and small useful things for workers. All of us needed workers on our plantations.

That was why three of my friends fixed up a ship for me to go to Africa. There I would trade for all of us. And so, that is how I came to that day which turned out to be so important in my life.

We had sailed only twelve days when a most terrible storm came up on us. Rain came down in curtains, making it dark all around. For days, the wind blew us every which way. Blankets of waves covered our ship and two men were washed overboard.

When the storm was past, we found we were near the mouth of the Orinoco River. Now we knew we were near a land of man – eating men! Thoughts of what could happen to us almost made us freeze.

As we crept along with our ship hurt by the storm, a second storm blew up. The waves were high around us when one of our men cried out, "Land!" Just then we felt that our ship had stopped moving. She was stuck on ground!

Thinking our ship would break into pieces within minutes, we hurried into our longboat. We were so afraid that our teeth were chattering. The sea was too stormy. In minutes, our boat was upside down. All we could do was swim for land.

I had to fight very hard to make it. The 30 foot waves washed me in and out. At last, I held fast to a big rock. Then I got up and out ran the next wave.

Safe on land, I looked back at our ship. It was so far out! I looked for the other men, but found only their hats and shoes!

I walked about, full of thanks for my life, feeling a great wonder that I was the only one safe. Then I remembered. Today was my birthday.

Eight Years Later—and ShipWrecked!!

COMPREHENSION CHECK

Choose the best answer.

1. The English captain took him to Africa where he learned
    _____ a. the way to Brazil.
    _____ b. how to fight the people.
    _____ c. to trade with the people.
    _____ d. to change dollars to pounds.

2. The pirate captain
    _____ a. gave him tables, beds, **and blankets.**
    _____ b. kept him in the north of **Africa.**
    _____ c. made him work hard.
    _____ d. helped him get away.

3. He got to Brazil by
    _____ a. sailing in his longboat.
    _____ b. getting picked up at sea.
    _____ c. by sailing with the pirates.
    _____ d. by getting away from the pirates.

4. In Brazil he
    _____ a. worked on a plantation.
    _____ b. traded ships for gold.
    _____ c. could go to sea as much as he wanted to.
    _____ d. owned a sugar plantation.

5. He was going from Brazil to Africa to get
    _____ a. workers for the   plantations.
    _____ b. back on the sea.
    _____ c. toys and bits of glass.
    _____ d. curtains for the longboat.

6. Thoughts that made them freeze, when they were near the mouth of the Orinoco River, were about
    _____ a. washing overboard.
    _____ b. being hurt.
    _____ c. being eaten.
    _____ d. getting stuck.

7. He got to land at last by
    _____ a. swimming.
    _____ b. rowing a longboat.
    _____ c. turning the boat upside down.
    _____ d. holding on to the boat.

8. He was full of thanks at the end of the story because he
    _____ a. still had his ship.
    _____ b. was full of wonder.
    _____ c. was not washed out to sea.
    _____ d. still had his life.

9. Another name for the story could be
    _____ a. "Getting Money in Brazil."
    _____ b. "Eight Years of Doing Nothing."
    _____ c. "To Africa, Brazil, and Back to Africa."
    _____ d. "Trading for Plantation Workers."

10. This story is mainly about
    _____ a. trading with Africa.
    _____ b. how he comes to be shipwrecked.
    _____ c. what life is like for a pirate on the sea.
    _____ d. why he should not have left England.

Check your answers with your answers with the key on page 67.

Eight Years Later—and ShipWrecked!

VOCABULARY CHECK

curtain	chatter	crept	blanket	freeze	enjoy

I. Sentences to Finish

Using the words in the big box above, choose the one which best fits in each of the sentences below. Write the words on the lines in the sentences.

1. As soon as the people got to the party, they began to _____ .

2. The snow covered the ground like a _____ .

3. It was so cold outside, the lake began to _____ .

4. As the _____ opened, the play began.

5. How I would _____ a tall glass of cold water!

6. The tiny baby _____ along, crawling on all fours.

II. Crossword Puzzle

Fill in the little boxes with the letters of the words at the top of the page. The numbers in the puzzle match the numbers of the meanings below. The meanings will help you guess which word fits each set of boxes.

Across

2. To talk quickly and a lot about things that are not important

3. A soft cover to keep you warm

4. To be happy with something

Down

1. To turn to ice

2. A cloth cover for a window

Check your answers with the key on page 69.

This page may be reproduced for classroom use.

17

Settling In

PREPARATION

Key Words

class	(klas)	a group of children with the same teacher *The teacher told the class to make a picture.* a group of people or things that are alike in some way, a kind of people or things *House cats are in the same class of animals as lions.* the grade of something *First class is the best way to go.*
crack	(krak)	begin to break something open or apart *There is a crack in this cup.* a sharp noise, made suddenly *The crack of thunder made us jump.* to break suddenly, with a sharp noise *The tree branch cracked from the heavy wind.*
finally	(fī′ nl ē)	at the end; at last *We finally found the book.* at the last point; in the end *After all that driving, we finally got to her house.* in such a way as to settle something; in a last way *I finally thought of an idea that would work well.*
hang	(hang)	place on a hook and let swing down from above *The swing will hang from a tree.* hold on to keep from falling *He was hanging on to the rope so he wouldn't hit the ground.*
replied	(rē plīd′)	answered *She replied, "Yes."*
thirty	(thėr′ tē)	three tens *There are thirty days in this month.* the number between 29 and 31 *He counted up to thirty, then stopped.*

 Settling In

Special Words

calendar	(kal′ ən dər)	table showing the months, weeks, and days of the year *I found my birthday on the calendar.*
fortress	(fôr′ tris)	a large fort or hide-away *The men built a fortress so that they would have a place to stay and be safe.*
mast	(mast)	a long pole of wood or metal set straight up to hold up the sails on a ship *The masts of ships can be seen from far away.*
oar	(ôr, ōr)	a long pole with one flat end, used in rowing *We got the boat across the lake by using oars.*
powder	(pou′ dər)	dry matter made into dust by pounding *Flour is a white powder made from grain and used to make bread.*
raft	(raft)	wood or boards put or tied together to make them float; used to move someone or something across water *The boy was out in the lake on a raft.*

Necessary Words

against	(ə genst′, ə gănst′)	opposite to; upon or toward; facing *The men leaned against the car to push it.*
barrel	(bar′ əl)	something that is round, with a flat top and bottom, its sides bend out a little; usually made of thick boards held together by metal bands, made to store things in *The farmer kept water in barrels.*
cave	(kāv)	hollow space under the ground, often with an opening in the side of a hill or mountain *Long ago, before they built houses, men lived in caves of rock.*
chain	(chān)	group of rings joined together; may be metal or other material; used to wrap or tie something up or hold it together *There is a chain with a lock on the gate to keep it closed.*
God	(god)	the special being honored in most religions as the maker and ruler of the world *No one can see God, but people all over the world pray to God.*
island	(ī′ lənd)	body of land with water all around it *Often islands are so far from the mainland that one must use a boat to go there.*
meat	(mēt)	animal flesh used as food, such as roasts or chops *I often cook a big piece of meat in the oven.*
mile	(mīl)	how far away someone or something may be; one mile is 5,280 feet *It takes me about twenty minutes to walk a mile.*
post	(pōst)	piece of wood, metal, or other material set up straight, usually to hold something up *The bird was sitting on the fence post.*
rat	(rat)	a long-tailed animal much like a mouse, but larger *Rats eat more things, destroy more, and are meaner than mice.*
settle	(set′ l)	to move into a place, to set up home somewhere *When we are settled in our new house, we will call you.*
Sunday	(sun′ dē, sun′ dā)	the first day of the week, a day of church and rest for many people *I always stay at home with my family on Sunday.*
tide	(tīd)	the flowing of water in and out in an ocean or stream *At high tide, the ocean comes all the way up on the beach.*
tool	(tül)	a knife, hammer, saw, shovel or any object used to help in doing work *The right tools makes it easier to do the work.*

Settling In

Robinson Crusoe built his fortress in a cave under a rocky hill. He used sails from the ship to make a tent going into the cave. He built a fence of two rows of posts of young trees. He pulled the ladder inside at night. Then he felt safe.

Preview:
1. Read the name of the story.
2. Look at the picture carefully.
3. Read the sentences under the picture.
4. Read the first three paragraphs of the story.
5. Then, answer the following question.

You learned from your preview
____ a.　that he got to land.
____ b.　how the ship was after the storm.
____ c.　that he got many things off the ship.
____ d.　that he made a raft to go to the ship.

Turn to the Comprehension Check on page 22 for the right answer.

Turn to the Comprehension Check on page 22 for the right answer.

Now read the story.

Read to find out how Robinson Cursoe made a home on the island.

 Settling In

When the storm was over, our ship had washed close to land and was still standing. If only we had all just stayed on board, everyone would have been safe!

It was an easy swim out to the ship. I pulled myself up by a rope. I sawed up the masts and tied them together to build a raft.

I let the raft hang from the side of the ship while I filled it with food, guns, tools, and trunks of clothes. When I let the raft down into the water, the tide was just coming in. It carried me right into the mouth of a little river.

Carefully, I waited for the water to come up higher and move me in over the land. Then I stuck the oars into the ground. When the tide went out, my raft sat on land.

In ten more trips I got everything I could off the ship — sails, nails, gun powder, ropes, chains, barrels of bread, money, and books. A dog and two cats came off, too. Then another storm made the ship crack up and washed it away.

Now to find a place for a fortress. It must be safe from wild animals and any man-eating men. It must be where I could watch out to sea for any ship. I found such a place way up a hill in front of a very large rock.

I set up my tent of sails against the big rock. Then, I made a strong fence all around the front. I made a ladder to go in and out. When I was inside, with my ladder pulled in, I finally felt safe.

I brought all my things into my fortress. Next, I started digging into a crack in the big rock to make a cave. Finally, I moved my things back into the cave. I used the tent as a doorway into it. All this I did in my first thirty days after the shipwreck.

Next, to see the country around me. From a hill top, I saw I was on an island, with the sea all around. About thirty miles away were some rocks sticking up. There were no signs of people anywhere.

I was all year building my fortress. It took three days for each tree in my fence. Part of every day, I went hunting for birds or goats for food.

To keep track of the days, I set up a large post. I made a cut in it for each day and a longer cut for every Sunday. This was my calendar.

Sometimes I felt very sorry for myself. But something inside me always replied, "But where are the other ten men? Is this not better?"

So I set myself to write down on paper the Bad and the Good. Under Bad, I put, "I am on an island, and can't get away." On the Good side, I put, "But I have life!"

Under Bad, I put, "I am alone." Under Good, I replied, "But God sent the ship near enough that I could get many things. I have everything I need or I can make it."

After that, I set to making things I needed. I made a table and chairs of boards. I made baskets of small branches so I could hang food up away from the dog and cats. Anything I wanted to do, I just thought about, quietly. Then I would know how to do it even if I had never had a teacher teach me in a class.

One day, I threw out a little corn the rats had got into on the ship. Later, I was surprised to see it grow. In time, I got the seed and planted it.

Another day, I walked to the other side of the island and found a large turtle. There were 60 eggs in her. My, they were good! And so was the meat of the turtle. That was high-class food!

Settling In

COMPREHENSION CHECK

> **Preview answer:**
>
> c.   that he got many things off the ship.

Choose the best answer.

1.   He made a raft from
  _____ a.   boards of the ship.
  _____ b.   the side of the ship.
  _____ c.   the masts tied together.
  _____ d.   ropes tied together.

2.   He was able to move the raft in the water by
  _____ a.   sticking oars into the ground.
  _____ b.   going with the tide.
  _____ c.   hanging it from the side of the ship.
  _____ d.   washing onto the land.

3.   He wanted a safe place to live away from
  _____ a.   any storms.
  _____ b.   large rocks.
  _____ c.   the dog and cats.
  _____ d.   man-eating men.

4.   After he had settled in, he went to see
  _____ a.   the people on the island.
  _____ b.   where he was.
  _____ c.   the ship break up.
  _____ d.   where the other 10 men were.

5.   His calendar was
  _____ a.   cuts in a large post.
  _____ b.   brought from the ship.
  _____ c.   printed on paper.
  _____ d.   rocks in the ground.

6.   He put down on paper good things and bad things so that he
  _____ a.   would know what to do next.
  _____ b.   could get or make everything he needed.
  _____ c.   could feel better about being alone on the island.
  _____ d.   would not feel bad about the other 10 men.

7.   He learned how to do things
  _____ a.   from writing it down on paper.
  _____ b.   from a book he took from the ship.
  _____ c.   in class from a teacher.
  _____ d.   by thinking what was the best way to do them.

8.   When he found the turtle, he
  _____ a.   took it to his fortress.
  _____ b.   gave it some corn.
  _____ c.   cooked and ate it.
  _____ d.   kept it for eggs.

9.   Another name for the story could be
  _____ a.   "I Make a Home on the Island."
  _____ b.   "Getting Everything Off the Ship."
  _____ c.   "Another Storm Washes My Ship Away."
  _____ d.   "Feeling Sorry for Myself."

10.   This story is mainly about
  _____ a.   finding a safe place to live on the island.
  _____ b.   being happy he was not washed out to sea.
  _____ c.   finding out how to be alone.
  _____ d.   making a home out of what he has.

Check your answers with the key on page 67.

VOCABULARY CHECK

crack	finally	hang	class	thirty	replied

I. Sentences to Finish

Using the words in the big box above, choose the one which best fits in each of the sentences below. Write the words on the lines in the sentences.

1. Three tens is the same as _____ .

2. Children who have the same teacher are in the same _____ .

3. When you put something on a hook, you let it _____ .

4. The gun made a loud _____ when it was shot.

5. When everything was ready, we _____ got started on our trip.

6. When I asked how she was, she _____ with a smile.

II. Words of Same Meaning

From the box above, choose the word which means the same as the one(s) underlined in each sentence. Write the one you chose on the line after the sentences.

1. My <u>group</u> was having an art lesson. _____

2. We will <u>put up</u> new curtains in our living room windows. _____

3. <u>Twenty and ten</u> people were in the bus. _____

4. I felt bad when I saw the <u>break</u> in the car window. _____

5. When I sent my letter, he <u>answered</u> by return mail. _____

6. <u>At last</u>, the rain stopped. _____

Check your answers with the key on page 69.

This page may be reproduced for classroom use.

I Find Peace — and Grow to be Happy

PREPARATION

Key Words

desk   (desk)

table at which you do your work
Each child in the room has a desk to work at.
a special kind of table for doing school work
My desk is in the front of the classroom.
a table with a smooth top just high enough for writing on
He sat at a desk to write a letter to his friend.

hall   (hôl)

a way to go through a building
We walked down the hall to get to her room.
the place between rooms in a building
Our classroom is across the hall from the front office.
place to walk from room to room
In my house I have to go through the hall to get to the kitchen.

jar   (jär)

glass with a wide mouth to store things in
She put the soup in the jar.
something like a jug with a wide mouth; may be made of glass, stone, clay, or plastic
Indians make beautiful clay jars by hand.

job   (job)

work that someone has to do
He had the job of painting the house.
work done for pay
Most people need jobs to make money.

sidewalk   (sīd' wôk')

place to walk at the side of a street
It is safe to walk on the sidewalk, not on the street.

special   (spesh' əl)

not like others
I have a special gift for you.
for a certain person, thing, reason
The library showed special films on weekends for children who go to school.
thought highly of, great, chief
He was a special worker because he did his job above and beyond what was asked of him.

I Find Peace — and Grow to be Happy

Special Words

deliver   (di liv′ ər)   set free, save
After he began thanking God, Robinson Crusoe was delivered of his feeling of guilt.

guilt   (gilt)   a feeling of having done wrong
Mr. Smith had feelings of guilt when he thought about how he shouted at the child.

parrot   (par′ ət)   a bird with a big, hooked bill and bright colored feathers that can sometimes copy sounds of words and sentences from people
You can often train parrots to say what you say.

prayer   (prar)   a form of words used to talk to God, to ask from God
Prayer helps us believe we will have the good we deeply want.

raisin   (rā′ zn)   a sweet dried grape
Raisins are good to eat for a snack.

tobacco   (tə bak′ ō)   a plant whose leaves are dried and used for smoking or chewing
Cigarettes and cigars are made of tobacco.

Necessary Words

also   (ôl′ sō)   add to, besides
That plant is pretty and also easy to grow!

Bible   (bī′ bəl)   a special book of writings of the Christian religion
We read a Bible to better understand God.

die   (dī)   stop living, no longer alive
The tree will die if it does not receive water.

dream   (drēm)   something thought, felt, or seen in sleep
I had a dream about a warm, sunny place, where there were many flowers.

dry   (drī)   not wet, not damp
When fruit is put in the sun, the juice dries out of it.

fast   (fast)   go without food; go without some special food
Robinson Crusoe fasted and prayed to give thanks to God.

forgive   (fər giv′)   not having hard or bad feelings at or toward someone; to give up the wish to hurt someone for doing wrong
When you don't forgive someone, you feel bad.

grape   (grāp)   a small, round, berrylike fruit that is red, purple, or pale-green, and grows in bunches on vines; when dried, they become raisins
My grandmother grows grapes in her yard.

hid   (hid)   covered up; out of sight
The clouds hid the sun.

mind   (mīnd)   the part of a person that knows, thinks, and feels
He has a quick mind; he could answer the question right away.

peace   (pēs)   a feeling of quiet; calm
I find peace in watching a sun set.

rum   (rum)   a drink made from sugar cane and molasses
Some people put rum in hot tea when they have a cold.

season   (sē′ zn)   four times of the year — spring, summer, autumn, winter
My favorite seasons are summer and autumn.

weak   (wēk)   not strong of body or mind
The dog was weak after spending three days out in the cold.

I Find Peace — and Grow to be Happy

When Robinson Crusoe was very sick, he found his Bible. He read it every day and soon came to be at peace. Then he did many things to make his life on the island more pleasant.

Preview: 1.   Read the name of the story.
                  2.   Look at the picture carefully.
                  3.   Read the sentences under the picture.
                  4.   Read the first paragraph of the story.
                  5.   Then, answer the following question.

You learned from your preview that Robinson Crusoe
_____ a.   had many bad dreams.
_____ b.   was very sick.
_____ c.   had trouble sleeping.
_____ d.   was in a great long hall.

Turn to the Comprehension Check on page 28 for the right answer.

Now read the story.

Read to find out what happened after Robinson Crusoe got sick.

I Find Peace — and Grow to be Happy

In that first summer, I was taken very sick. For days, I had long fits of being freezing cold, followed by feeling very hot. I grew very weak. My head got so stopped up that I felt I was down in the corner of a big hall.

When I could finally get some sleep, I had a terrible dream. I saw a man in flashing fire come from the black sky. He said, "Seeing all these things have not brought you to me, now you shall die!"

The next day I kept thinking, "What am I? Where did all this world come from?" The answer followed, "God made it. And he cares for everything in it."

Then I thought about how I had been made safe through two shipwrecks and my time under the pirates. Still, I had never turned my mind to thank God.

I went to a trunk to get some tobacco to put in a jar of rum and water to help me get well. In the trunk, I also found help for my troubled mind — a Bible. I sat down at my desk table to read. My eyes fell on, "Call on me in the day of trouble and I will deliver you."

I took a drink of rum with tobacco, and went to bed. I fell into a deep sleep until the next afternoon. After that, I grew stronger each day.

My thoughts kept running to the Bible words, "I will deliver you." But how could I ever get off this island? Then the thought came, "But God had delivered you from being terribly sick." At this, I started thanking God out loud.

Every day, I sat at my desk or lay in my bed and read the Bible. Soon I came to think of the words, "I will deliver you," in a different way. I had long carried a deep feeling of guilt. To be delivered from this feeling would be wonderful! I read, "I am come to forgive you." And then a great peace came over me.

Now I made up my mind to make my way of living as nice as I could. I wanted to see what else was on my island. As I went out walking with my gun and dog, I really did not miss the sidewalks of London.

I found beautiful fields of grass and many fruits, oranges and such. I hung grapes up on tree branches to dry into raisins. I had enough to fill many jars and baskets.

I found an opening in the woods that was like a great hall with trees all around. Here I set up another tent and fence. I called this my country home. Building it was not near such a job as building my fortress.

My calendar post told me it was September again. I had been on my island all of one year. To remember my landing, I made September 30 a special day. I fasted and prayed, giving thanks that I was safe.

By keeping track in my day book, I began to see that my island had two rainy seasons and two dry seasons.

I found the best time of the year to grow corn by planting some at two different times. The rain drowned the first little plants.

Surprise! My fence posts began growing! Their bushy branches soon hid my houses. And with no sidewalks showing the way to my homes, I felt safe in them.

On a trip across the island, I caught a parrot. Making a cage for it was a job much like making baskets.

On another trip, my dog caught a wild goat. I brought it home to try to keep it for milking. A few days without food made it so glad to see me that it followed me like a dog.

The second year went by quickly. Again, I kept September 30 as a special day of fasting and prayer. By this time, I had made up my mind that I could be really happy on my island.

I Find Peace — and Grow to be Happy

COMPREHENSION CHECK

Choose the best answer.

1. When he was sick, he
    _____ a.   would sleep all day.
    _____ b.   thought he might not live.
    _____ c.   had a dream about the shipwreck.
    _____ d.   met a man on the island.

2. Help for his troubled mind came from
    _____ a.   reading the Bible.
    _____ b.   writing at his desk.
    _____ c.   a jar of rum and water.
    _____ d.   getting some sleep.

3. When he read that God said he would be delivered, Robinson Crusoe knew he
    _____ a.   would read the Bible every day.
    _____ b.   would get back to London soon.
    _____ c.   would be all right.
    _____ d.   would never feel sick again.

4. He was able to have raisins by
    _____ a.   growing and picking them.
    _____ b.   filling jars and baskets with them.
    _____ c.   hanging grapes up to dry.
    _____ d.   looking in the woods for them.

5. His country home was
    _____ a.   a tent in the woods.
    _____ b.   his fortress.
    _____ c.   in a great hall.
    _____ d.   hard to build.

6. The fence posts
    _____ a.   were made into sidewalks.
    _____ b.   were used by his parrot.
    _____ c.   were used for the tent.
    _____ d.   grew into bushy trees.

7. When his dog caught the wild goat, Robinson Crusoe
    _____ a.   made a cage for it.
    _____ b.   brought it home.
    _____ c.   gave it milk.
    _____ d.   killed and ate it.

8. At the end of the story, he was happy because
    _____ a.   he knew his island life was not so bad after all.
    _____ b.   another year was gone.
    _____ c.   he had a special day.
    _____ d.   he had a safe fortress and a nice country home.

9. Another name for the story could be
    _____ a.   "Getting Well."
    _____ b.   "I Take Time to Thank God and Find Peace."
    _____ c.   "I Find Jobs to Do."
    _____ d.   "My First Two Years on the Island."

10. This story is mainly about
    _____ a.   how he made a special day out of September 30.
    _____ b.   his knowing he will soon find a way off the island.
    _____ c.   how he found food on the island.
    _____ d.   his being able to see that his life was good.

Check your answers with the key on page 67.

I Find Peace — and Grow to be Happy

VOCABULARY CHECK

desk	hall	jar	job	sidewalk	special

I. Sentences to Finish

Using the words in the big box above, choose the one which best fits in each of the sentences below. Write the words on the lines in the sentences.

1. My birthday is a _____ day to me.

2. Please get the _____ of honey.

3. Clean off your _____ ; it is time to go home.

4. You did a beautiful _____ at your work.

5. The pictures along the _____ are pretty.

6. The _____ is wide in front of our school.

II. Matching

Draw a line to match each word with its meaning.

sidewalk	glass with a wide mouth to store things in
hall	place to walk at the side of a street
desk	work that someone has to do
jar	place between rooms
job	not like others
special	special table to write on

Check your answers with the key on page 70.

I Truly Work for my Bread

PREPARATION

Key Words

bench   (bench)   a long seat
I sat on the bench and waited for the bus.
a work table used by one who works with tools; a work bench
I will build a bird house at my work bench.

chance   (chans)   something that may happen; opportunity
Give Jimmy a chance to hit the ball.
a risk; something not sure
We always take a chance when we do something new.

coach   (kōch)   someone who teaches or trains people to play a game
A good coach helps the players to do their best.
being taught or shown how to do something, or do it better
The teacher will coach us on how the drawing is done.

lose   (lüz)   not have any longer, fail to keep
If I lose the keys, I can't get in the house.
not win
Winning a game is fun, but losing is not.

team   (tēm)   a number of people working together
Our team did the cleaning while the others did the painting.
one of the sides in a game
In basketball, each team has five players on its side.

worry   (wėr' ē)   be a little bit afraid
I worry about being late when I sleep too long.
feeling uneasy; troubled
Worry about what might happen kept me from being happy.

I Truly Work for my Bread

Special Words

barley	(bär′ lē)	grain of a plant; its seeds, used for food *Some people put barley in soup.*
bran	(bran)	the broken coat of the grain of wheat; separated from the flour or meal and used in cereal, bread, and other foods *Bread with bran in it is very good for you.*
bushel	(bush′ əl)	unit for measuring grain and other dry things *A bushel of wheat is as much as 32 quarts.*
earth	(ėrth)	ground or dirt *Seeds should be planted in good, rich earth.*
rice	(rīs)	the grain of cereal grass grown in warm weather and forming one of the important foods of the world *I like to eat rice with chicken.*
scarf	(skärf)	a long, wide strip of cloth worn about a part of the body *He wore a scarf around his neck to keep warm.*

NOTE: All such grains as wheat, barley, and rice were called corn 300 years ago. At that time the grain we now call corn, was called maize.

Necessary Words

broke	(brōk)	came to pieces; fell apart *The window broke when a baseball hit it.*
dried	(drīd)	when food is empty of water or juice *Some stores sell both dried fruit and fresh fruit.*
earthen	(ėr′ thən)	made of baked clay; made of earth *American Indians make beautiful earthen pots.*
flat	(flat)	not very deep or thick *A plate is flat.*
grown	(grōn)	something that is at full size; does not have to be large *The dog is small, but she is full grown.*
hour	(our)	one of the 24 parts of time a day is made up of; 60 minutes *It took him three hours to finish his home work.*
month	(munth)	one of the twelve parts of the year; 30 or 31 days *Telephone bills are paid once a month.*
Poll	(pol)	the name given to Robinson Crusoe's parrot *Poll is short for the name of Polly.*
pot	(pot)	a round, rather deep container made of metal or earth *Many of our cooking pots are of iron or steel, but Robinson Crusoe's pots were earthen.*
raked	(rākt)	moved on the ground with a rake (long handled tool with a bar at one end, with teeth in the bar) *I cut the grass and then raked it all up.*
shake	(shāk)	to scatter by moving quickly from side to side *When you shake sand, the smaller grains go to the bottom and the larger ones come to the top.*
shaped	(shāpt)	formed into something, changed in shape *We shaped the batter into cookies.*
shot	(shot)	the act of shooting a gun; having pulled the trigger so that a ball of lead is fired from the gun *The hunter shot and killed a deer.*
thin	(thin)	easy to see through, light *The thin window curtains let in the sun light.*

31

I Truly Work for my Bread

When Robinson Crusoe lifted the earthen pot that made the top part of his oven, he saw that his bread had baked beautifully.

Preview: 1. Read the name of the story.
2. Look at the picture carefully.
3. Read the sentence under the picture.
4. Read the first paragraph of the story.
5. Then, answer the following question.

You learned from your preview that Robinson Crusoe
_____ a. got bread from the ship.
_____ b. got seed corn.
_____ c. lost his seed corn.
_____ d. may be able to bake bread.

Turn to the Comprehension Check on page 34 for the right answer.

Now read the story.

Read to find out how Robinson Crusoe got his bread.

I Truly Work for my Bread

My bread from the ship was gone. But I did have about ⅛ of a bushel of seed corn. If I could work out the ways and means, I might one day be able to bake bread. But I must not lose my seed!

I took a chance and planted the barley and rice. The young plants were beautiful. Then came the birds! I shot three and put them up in the field. At night, my dog kept watch. After that, I didn't have to worry; not another bird came. My dog and I made such a good team that I grew 36 times as much corn as I had planted. I stored it all for seed, in baskets on a bench in my cave.

To plant the new seed, I had to make ready much more land. First, I turned up the earth with a wooden shovel. Then, I raked the seed into the ground with heavy tree branches. When the corn was grown, I cut and dried it. Then, I hit it against a big rock to get the seeds out.

But before that, I needed more things to store it in. I set my mind to make some pots and jars. First, I found the right kind of earth. I shaped it into pots and set them to dry in the sun. With no coach to show me anything, I lost a lot. As they dried, they broke! In two months, I had two strange looking earthen jars. Very carefully, I set them on my bench.

In the house, when it was raining, I tried to teach my parrot to talk. He soon called out his name, "Poll." This was the first word I had heard from any mouth but my own in over two years! That made me feel like I had a new one on my team. The parrot sat and talked as I worked.

I still needed pots to cook in. One day I found in the fire, a broken piece of a jar, hard as stone. This made me take a chance on burning some new pots. I piled my sun-dried earthen pots onto live hot coals. I put firewood around and on top. I made a roaring fire until the pots were red-hot, and kept them that way for six hours. Then, all night long, I made the fire smaller and smaller, a little at a time. By morning, I had five good cooking pots.

My next job was to get my barley and rice ground into flour. I settled on using a great block of very hard wood. I burned out a hole in the top of it. I shaped a piece of wood to fit the hole. Then, I put in barley or rice and ground it into flour!

The hardest thing to work out was how to get the bran out of the flour. Finally, I thought about a thin neck scarf. I found I could shake the flour through, and the bran would stay in the scarf.

Now, to bake the bread. How to make an oven? Oh, if I only had someone to coach me! But finally, I thought it out myself. I made a wide earthen pot, not too deep, to turn upside down over my bread. I fired some flat pieces to lay the bread on.

To ready my oven for baking, I set down the flat pieces. I raked live coals onto them until they were hot through. Then, I cleaned away the coals, set down my bread, and turned my big wide pot over the bread. I covered it all with hot coals. I had the best barley bread and rice cakes any oven in the world could bake!

This time when I gathered my corn, I had 20 bushels of barley and 20 of rice. This was much more than I could eat in a year. So, I began to use it as much as I wanted. I would never have to worry about losing it again!

I Truly Work for my Bread

COMPREHENSION CHECK

Choose the best answer.

1. Until this story, his bread had come from
    ____ a. planting barley and rice.
    ____ b. a bushel of seed corn.
    ____ c. the wrecked ship.
    ____ d. cooking it in an oven.

2. He and his dog made a good team
    ____ a. keeping birds away.
    ____ b. planting seeds.
    ____ c. finding goats.
    ____ d. making jars from earth.

3. He had trouble making pots at first because
    ____ a. he had never done it before.
    ____ b. the earth for making pots was not good.
    ____ c. there was not enough wood to make a fire.
    ____ d. they broke as they dried in the sun.

4. He was happy when Poll could talk to him because
    ____ a. he wanted another one for his team.
    ____ b. he was sad without other people.
    ____ c. he had nothing else to do when it was raining but talk to Poll.
    ____ d. he had heard no one talk in two years.

5. He learned how to make pots to cook with by
    ____ a. having someone coach him.
    ____ b. taking a chance.
    ____ c. thinking about it quietly.
    ____ d. reading how to do it.

6. He ground barley and rice into flour
    ____ a. by using one piece of wood that fit into a hole in a block of wood.
    ____ b. by warming them on hot coals.
    ____ c. by shaking them through a thin neck scarf.
    ____ d. fitting them through a hole in a piece of wood.

7. He baked the bread
    ____ a. in a big wide bed of hot coals.
    ____ b. in an earthen oven covered by hot coals.
    ____ c. on flat pieces put on top of coals.
    ____ d. on hot coals with flat pieces on top.

8. The 20 bushels of barley and 20 bushels of rice he gathered were
    ____ a. what he had a chance to lose in a year.
    ____ b. as much as he wanted.
    ____ c. as much as he needed in a year.
    ____ d. more than he needed for a year.

9. Another name for the story could be
    ____ a. "Life is Hard."
    ____ b. "I Grow More Rice and Barley Than I Need."
    ____ c. "I Never Have to Worry About Bread Again."
    ____ d. "Someone to Talk To."

10. This story is mainly about
    ____ a. how seeds grow into plants.
    ____ b. how to make bread.
    ____ c. how he found a way to have bread year after year.
    ____ d. how he could make a good life from farming.

Check your answers with the key on page 67.

I Truly Work for my Bread

VOCABULARY CHECK

bench	chance	coach	lose	team	worry

I. Sentences to Finish

Using the words in the big box above, choose the one which best fits in each of the sentences below. Write the words on the lines in the sentences.

1. "I _____ when you're late," said Mother.

2. The _____ shouted, "Keep your eyes on the ball!"

3. Soon Jack will be tall enough to be on the basketball _____ .

4. A squirrel jumped on the _____ where I sat.

5. We stood in line and waited for a _____ to get a drink.

6. It is not easy to _____ and still believe in yourself.

II. Words In Sentences

Cross out the word that does not belong.

1. I hope our school (team, coach) wins the prize.

2. Give me a (worry, chance) to talk!

3. You know you can do it, so don't (lose, worry).

4. Mr. Gray, the (coach, team), helped us give a good play.

5. We made a new (bench, coach) in our workshop.

6. It is important to not (team, lose) track of what you are trying to do.

Check your answers with the key on page 70.

This page may be reproduced for classroom use.

Quiet Happenings—and Frightening!

PREPARATION

Key Words

chew	(chü)	to keep biting on something *When we eat, we should chew our food well.* use the teeth, or tooth-like parts, to break something up, make it smaller *The dog chewed on the bone.*
dash	(dash)	to run quickly *The cat dashed up a tree to get away from a dog.* hit or throw very hard; hard enough to hurt or break *The waves dashed Robinson Crusoe against the rocks.*
meant	(ment)	to have had in mind *He meant to help.* to have planned to do *Bob meant to play baseball, but his friends wanted to play football.* intended *The little boat was not meant to go so far.*
meat	(mēt)	the parts of animals and plants that are eaten *Some animals like to eat the meat of nuts.* animal flesh used as food, such as **roasts** or chops *Beef and pork are meats most people like.*
rid	(rid)	to do away with *Mother wants to get rid of the old clothes.* be free of *I want to be rid of this useless thing.*
spoil	(spoil)	to be hurt by always getting what you want; to harm *You can spoil a pet if you don't teach it to do what is right.* when food goes bad; becomes not fit to eat *The eggs spoiled from being in the heat too long.*

Quiet Happenings—and Frightening!

Special Words

comfortably	(kum′ fər tə blē)	in an easy way, free from hurt or sadness *She lives <u>comfortably</u>, with everything she really wants.*
current	(kér′ ənt)	a flow of water or air *The <u>current</u> carried the logs down the river.*
herd	(hėrd)	a group of animals of one kind, such as horses, elephants, or other large animals *We saw a <u>herd</u> of cows on the ranch.*
loose	(lüs)	not fastened or joined, not tight *The coat was so big, it was <u>loose</u> on me.*
umbrella	(um brel′ ə)	a light, round cover on a pole or stick used to keep the rain, sun or wind off someone or something *I brought my <u>umbrella</u> to work with me, in case it rains.*
valuable	(val′ ẏu ə bəl, val′ yə bəl)	being worth something; useful, special, or costing a lot *The old ring is very <u>valuable</u>.*

Necessary Words

cheese	(chēz)	a solid food made from the thick part of milk *Many different kinds of <u>cheese</u> are made in different countries.*
fan	(fan)	to stir the air, to make a breeze *He used a piece of board to <u>fan</u> the fire.*
ink	(ingk)	a black or colored liquid used for writing, painting, or drawing *I like to draw with <u>ink</u>.*
joy	(joi)	a strong feeling of happiness or gladness *The man was full of <u>joy</u> when he got what he had wanted.*
main	(mān)	most important, chief, largest *The offices are the <u>main</u> building.*
pants	(pants)	clothing that is worn on the legs *The boy was wearing black <u>pants</u> and a white shirt.*
pen	(pen)	a small, closed yard for animals *Chickens are kept in a <u>pen</u>.*
pit	(pit)	a hole in the ground usually made by digging *The <u>pit</u> was so deep you could not get out without a ladder.*
sand	(sand)	tiny grains of rock that has been worn down by water or wind *<u>Sand</u> is found in deserts and on beaches.*
sight	(sīt)	that which can be seen *I lost <u>sight</u> of the airplane when it was in the clouds.*
skin	(skin)	the dried outer layer of tissue from an animal that has been killed; animal hide *The hunter used animal <u>skins</u> to make a coat.*
smoke	(smōk)	that which is smoked, usually tobacco in a cigarette, cigar, or pipe *They wanted a <u>smoke</u> after dinner.*
vegetable	(vej′ ə tə bəl, vej′ tə bəl)	a plant whose fruit, stems, roots, or other parts are used for food, such as peas, lettuce, and potatoes *We usually have meat and <u>vegetables</u> for supper.*

Quiet Happenings—and Frightening!

After 15 years of being alone and safe on his island, Robinson Crusoe saw a foot print in the sand. It had been made by a man larger than he, but he did not know what kind of a man or where he was. He was very frightened!

Preview:
1. Read the name of the story.
2. Look at the picture carefully.
3. Read the sentences under the picture.
4. Read the first two paragraphs of the story.
5. Then, answer the following question.

You learned from your preview that Robinson Crusoe

_____ a. went to the main land.

_____ b. wanted to go to England.

_____ c. fixed up the old life boat.

_____ d. got his new boat into the water.

Turn to the Comprehension Check on page 40 for the right answer.

Now read the story

Read to find out if Robinson Crusoe made a boat he could use.

Quiet Happenings—and Frightening!

Time and again I thought of the mainland 40 miles away. If only I were there, I might get a ship back to England. Some way, I meant to get there.

Our ship's life boat had washed in. But no way could I move it. So, I made a fine big boat from a large tree trunk. But digging a waterway to bring it out, would take me ten years! I just had to give up the idea.

On September 30, my main thought was that the only things valuable to us are the ones we can use. I had piles of money, but it was of no use. I would gladly have traded it for vegetable seeds, a bottle of ink, and a tobacco pipe. For four years, I could only chew tobacco. How I would enjoy a smoke!

Also, I thought of how many times we spoil being happy by not giving thanks for what we have. I pictured myself without all the things from our ship.

My clothes were wearing out; I might as well be rid of them. From the dried skins of the animals I had killed for meat, I made a hat, coat, and pants. They were big and loose to catch and fan the air. The hair on the outside kept off the rain. I also made an umbrella for keeping off both the rain and sun.

For the next five years, I lived very comfortably. The most important thing I did was to make a boat of a smaller tree trunk. I fitted my boat with a mast and sail, and fixed my umbrella at the back. I put on board dried meat, raisins, and tobacco to chew. My little boat was not meant to go to the mainland.

I set out to go around my island. I soon came to a great rocky point that took me over six miles out to sea. The strong currents that caught my little boat took me even farther. I was lucky to not be dashed against the rocks. Just as I was so far out that I was about to lose all sight of my island, a little wind blew up. Quickly, I set my sail. Then I was carried out of that current and into another, running back. With this, I came to the other side of my island, safe and sound.

I tied my boat in the mouth of a little river and left it. I would never try to go around that rocky point again.

I got rid of the idea of going to sea. I set my mind to doing things better. I made better pots and different baskets. And, oh joy! I made an earthen pipe for tobacco.

I made a pitfall to catch goats. I put barley in the big hole and covered it over with branches. When the goats walked on the branches, they fell in. I fenced pens to keep my goats near my country home. In three years I had a herd large enough to keep me in meat, milk, butter, and cheese.

I had now been on my island 15 years. I had been very busy making and building things. Now, my main job was to keep fixing my fences and to be sure everything was safe.

One day, while going to see about my boat, I was greatly surprised. There in the sand was a print of a man's foot! I stopped as if I had been hit by something out of the sky. I listened. I looked around. Nothing. I went up on a little hill. Still nothing. I came back to the footprint. Was it real? Yes, every part of a man's foot print was there. My mind went wild! And my feet flew. Dashing all the way across the island, back into my fortress, they hardly hit the ground.

Worry spoiled any sleep. "What kind of man made that footprint? And where is he now?" I didn't chance leaving my fortress for three days.

Quiet Happenings—and Frightening!

COMPREHENSION CHECK

Choose the best answer.

1. He could get back to England if he could
    ____ a. get to the main land.
    ____ b. make a boat to get there by sea.
    ____ c. find the ship's lifeboat.
    ____ d. dig out a large tree trunk.

2. On September 30, he thought of how
    ____ a. happy he was to have piles of money.
    ____ b. useful were the things from the ship.
    ____ c. happy he would have been living in London.
    ____ d. he had no need for clothes.

3. He used his umbrella
    ____ a. to keep off the rain and sun.
    ____ b. for a mast and a sail.
    ____ c. to catch and fan the air.
    ____ d. as a hat and coat.

4. Trying to go around the island, he
    ____ a. lost sight of land.
    ____ b. was carried out to sea by the current.
    ____ c. was dashed against the rocks in the sea.
    ____ d. was lost at sea.

5. Because he was afraid of going out in his boat again, he
    ____ a. worked with his goats all day.
    ____ b. took walks around the island.
    ____ c. rid his mind of going to sea.
    ____ d. dried meats and raisins all day.

6. The goats were caught when they
    ____ a. fell into a pit.
    ____ b. went near his country home.
    ____ c. ran into his fence.
    ____ d. fell on the branches.

7. He was afraid when he saw the foot print because he
    ____ a. had not seen a man in so long.
    ____ b. did not know what a man might be doing there.
    ____ c. knew the man would take what he had.
    ____ d. did not want someone there after so many years.

8. Worry spoiled his sleep because
    ____ a. he had been hit by something out of the sky.
    ____ b. he dashed home all the way across the island.
    ____ c. he did not leave his fortress.
    ____ d. he was afraid his island was not safe.

9. Another name for the story could be
    ____ a. "I Go to Sea Again."
    ____ b. "My Thoughts Go Back to England."
    ____ c. "I Try to Keep My Island Safe and Happy."
    ____ d. "15 Years on the Island."

10. This story is mainly about
    ____ a. what his life was like on the island for many years.
    ____ b. finally finding another man on the island.
    ____ c. his wanting to be home again.
    ____ d. his almost getting into another ship-wreck.

Check your answers with the key on page 67.

Quiet Happenings—and Frightening!

VOCABULARY CHECK

chew	dash	meant	meat	rid	spoil

I. Sentences to Finish

Using the words in the big box above, choose the one which best fits in each of the sentences below. Write the words on the lines in the sentences.

1. We _____ food when we eat it.

2. Sometimes we eat _____ for dinner.

3. We _____ children when we give them everything they want without their working for it.

4. He said one thing, but he _____ another.

5. It was raining so hard that we had to _____ into the house.

6. We had to get _____ of the dog when it bit the baby.

II. Cross Word Puzzle

Fill in the little boxes with the letters of the words at the top of the page. The numbers in the puzzle match the numbers of the meanings below. The meanings will help you guess which word fits each set of boxes.

Across

2. Beef and pork we eat
4. To go bad

Down

1. To run fast
2. To have had in mind
3. To throw away

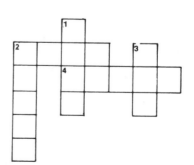

Check your answers with the key on page 70.

This page may be reproduced for classroom use.

Cannibals on my Island!

PREPARATION

Key Words

fur	(fėr)	soft hair that covers some animals *The cat's fur coat keeps him warm on cold days.* animal skin with its hair covering, dried and dressed to make it soft *Fur coats are very warm and comfortable.*
mile	(mīl)	a long way; about 20 city blocks long *We walked a mile to the park.* a measure of distance or length; 5,280 feet *My friend and I walked three miles in an hour.*
moment	(mō' mənt)	a very short bit of time; not as long as a minute *John missed the train, because he was a moment late.* at the same time *We got to school at the same moment.* just as soon as *The moment the sun came up, the birds started singing.*
rule	(rül)	a saying that tells us what to do and what not to do *One basketball rule is "No pushing."* set of sentences that tell what is right and what is wrong *The Bible gives rules to live by.* a thing that happens or is done most of the time *As a rule, it is very warm in summer.*
rush	(rush)	to move fast *Mrs. Brown rushed to the store before it closed.* come, go, pass, or act very fast *He rushes into things without thinking.* send, push, or carry very fast *Please rush this mail.* hurry *Don't rush around so; you will knock things over.*
sidewalk	(sīd' wôk')	place to walk at the side of a street *In the city, people walk on the sidewalk, not in the road.* a narrow lane, made like a road, but only for walking *The sidewalk in front of my house is made of the same thing as the street.*

Cannibals on my Island!

Special Words

cannibal (kan′ ə bəl) a person who eats human flesh as meat
There are <u>cannibals</u> in some parts of the world.

disgust (dis gust′) strong dislike
I felt great <u>disgust</u> when I saw the two women fighting.

feast (fēst) a big meal for a special day or happening
We had a big <u>feast</u> when my sister got married.

flesh (flesh) the meat of the body that covers the bones and is covered by the skin
When you are fat you have lots of <u>flesh</u>.

scattered (skat′ ərd) thrown here and there, spread around
The pieces from the puzzle were <u>scattered</u> all over the table.

telescope (tel′ ə skōp) a special tube to look through, that makes things that are far away seem closer and bigger
You can use a <u>telescope</u> at the beach to see the big boats out at sea.

Necessary Words

added (ad′ əd) joined to something, put with something
We <u>added</u> a new room to our house.

blood (blud) red liquid moved within the body by the heart, carrying air and food to all parts of the body and carrying away waste matter
There was a lot of <u>blood</u> on my hand when I cut it.

built (bilt) having made something, such as houses, ships, stores, bridges
My brother <u>built</u> a tree house in the big old oak tree.

dead (ded) no longer living; that has died
The man was <u>dead</u> from drowning.

dripping (drip′ ing) being so wet that drops fall
When I came in out of the rain, I was <u>dripping</u>.

fear (fir) a feeling that harm or something bad is near or about to happen
Strong <u>fear</u> can make you sick.

hidden (hid′ n) put or kept somewhere so as not to be seen
The candy was <u>hidden</u> somewhere in the kitchen.

mine (mīn) the one or ones belonging to me
That book is <u>mine</u>; I bought it at the book store.

shore (shôr, shōr) land at the edge of a sea, lake or other body of water
The group sat on the <u>shore</u> and watched the swimmers.

upon (ə pôn′, ə pon′) on
I set the dish <u>upon</u> the table.

Cannibals on my Island!

When he saw the light of a fire, Robinson Crusoe climbed to the top of the hill above his fortress where he could see what was going on. Through his telescope, he watched the cannibals having a merry-making feast on the shore about two miles away.

Preview:
1. Read the name of the story.
2. Look at the picture carefully.
3. Read the sentences under the picture.
4. Read the first two paragraphs of the story.
5. Then, answer the following question.

You learned from your preview that Robinson Crusoe
_____ a. could sleep until morning.
_____ b. was sick from fear.
_____ c. found a foot print.
_____ d. made a larger foot print.

Turn to the Comprehension Check on page 46 for the right answer.

Now read the story.

Read to find out about the cannibals.

Cannibals on my Island!

Fear is terrible! I shook. I was hot, then cold. After five days, I went back to the footprint to see if I might have made it. But no, it was much larger than mine.

I rushed home again, feeling so afraid that I couldn't think straight. It was almost morning before I could sleep. As I woke up, I remembered the Bible words, "Call on me in the day of trouble and I will deliver you."

I began to think. "I have lived here 15 years without seeing a sign of another man. The thing for me to do is to make my fortress a safe place to run to if ever I do see a cannibal."

So, I built a second wall with seven guns set in it. I could fire them all in two minutes.

I saw nothing more for three years. Then, along the shore, I came upon a most terrible sight. Bones of people — head, leg, and arm bones — were scattered around a fire pit! Thoughts of the terrible feast made me so sick that I threw up.

Night and day I thought about how I might kill the cannibals if I saw them. But after three months, I began to think it was not right for me to kill them. They had never learned *not* to eat men. And it was not up to me to set rules of right and wrong for them. After all, they were not trying to kill me. My job was to keep myself and my houses hidden. Having no sidewalks helped.

Later, many times I was glad that I had not tried to kill the cannibals. I thought about the many times in my life that I had followed a secret feeling deep in my mind. Always, it had turned out to be the best rule for me to follow.

Keeping safe was the biggest thing on my mind. One day, I found a cave with an opening big enough to stand in. But then I saw two large shiny eyes. For a moment, I couldn't move; then I rushed out. A lighted stick showed only an old goat. He was so frightened of me that his fur stood up!

I crawled about ten feet inside the cave and found a large room. The walls were shiny and the floor dry. What a great place to store my gun powder!

After 22 years on my island, I was surprised one morning by the light of a fire. It was on my side of the island about two miles away! As I lay down flat on top of my hill, I looked through my telescope and saw cannibals dancing. The moment the tide came in, they rowed off in their boats.

I carried so many guns that it took me two hours to walk the two miles. And walking through the woods was not like walking on sidewalks. Around the fire pit, I saw prints where 20 or more men had been sitting.

Scattered around the fire pit were blood, bones, and pieces of men's flesh left from their merry making. I was filled with such disgust that I began again to want to kill the cannibals. But I did not see them again for more than a year.

In May, a great storm wrecked a ship at the rocky point of my island. Only one man washed on shore — dead. "Oh, that he had lived!" How nice it would have been to have some one with me.

From the ship, I got money, clothing, shoes, a fire shovel, cooking pots, and some good hard candies. The best thing was a dog. When he saw me, he came swimming. His fur dripping with water, I gladly helped him into my boat. My old dog had died after 16 years with me.

The things I got from the ship added little joys to my living. I felt easy enough. Only, I was more watchful. And I kept mostly to my part of the island.

Cannibals on my Island!

COMPREHENSION CHECK

Choose the best answer.

1. He rushed back to his fortress
   ____ a.　to make his fortress safe.
   ____ b.　to go to sleep.
   ____ c.　because he couldn't think straight.
   ____ d.　because he was afraid.

2. Scattered around a fire pit was (were)
   ____ a.　a terrible feast.
   ____ b.　cannibal bones.
   ____ c.　pieces of wood and stones.
   ____ d.　bones of men who had been eaten.

3. He knew it was not right to kill the cannibals because
   ____ a.　they were the first men he had seen.
   ____ b.　it is always wrong to kill.
   ____ c.　they did not know they were doing wrong.
   ____ d.　they had let him live.

4. After three months of thinking about the cannibals, he thought he should
   ____ a.　set up rules of right and wrong for them.
   ____ b.　keep himself hidden.
   ____ c.　try to kill them.
   ____ d.　cover over his sidewalks.

5. The fur standing up on the old goat showed that
   ____ a.　the goat was afraid of him.
   ____ b.　he was afraid of the goat.
   ____ c.　the lighted stick gave a lot of light.
   ____ d.　it was cold in the cave.

6. When he saw what was left of the terrible feast,
   ____ a.　he did not want to see cannibals again for a year.
   ____ b.　he again wanted to kill all the cannibals.
   ____ c.　he rushed to his fortress to make it safe.
   ____ d.　he got sick at what had happened.

7. When he saw that the man from the shipwreck had washed on shore,
   ____ a.　he thought the cannibals had killed him.
   ____ b.　he wished the man had lived.
   ____ c.　he knew the man was dead.
   ____ d.　he was afraid there were others around.

8. The best thing he found from the ship that was wrecked was
   ____ a.　a new boat.
   ____ b.　money.
   ____ c.　clothes and shoes.
   ____ d.　a dog.

9. Another name for this story could be
   ____ a.　"22 Years on My Island."
   ____ b.　"ManEaters Have Been Here."
   ____ c.　"Another Shipwreck."
   ____ d.　"I Become Sick Again."

10. This story is mainly about
   ____ a.　his being afraid of cannibals.
   ____ b.　him seeing terrible sights.
   ____ c.　him finding a dog.
   ____ d.　knowing what is right and wrong.

Check your answers with the key on page 67.

Cannibals on my Island!

VOCABULARY CHECK

| fur | mile | moment | rule | rush | sidewalk |

I. Sentences to Finish

Using the words in the big box above, choose the one which best fits in each of the sentences below. Write the words on the lines in the sentences.

1. "Cross at the green, not in between," is a good _____ to follow.

2. The _____ I saw that puppy, I knew it was the one for me.

3. A _____ hat is warm.

4. I asked the store to _____ the things I bought.

5. The ground was so muddy that I was happy to have a _____ to walk on.

6. The railroad is about a _____ from my house.

II. Matching

Draw a line to match each word with its meaning.

fur   a very short time

mile   things to do and not do

moment   hurry

rule   place to walk beside a street

rush   animal skins

sidewalk   measure used to tell how far it is from one town to another

Check your answers with the key on page 71.

My Man, Friday!

PREPARATION

Key Words

already	(ôl red′ ē)	before this time; by this time *The boy has already broken his truck.* before now *The job has already been done.*
boots	(büts)	covers for the feet and legs to keep them dry *Put on your boots to keep your feet dry.* a kind of shoe that has high sides to cover the ankle and often the leg, too *I like to wear boots when it is cold.*
cave	(kāv)	an empty hole in the ground *We hid in a cave and no one could find us.* hollow space under the ground, often with an opening in the side of a hill or mountain *Long ago, before men learned to build houses, they lived in caves.*
eager	(ē′ gər)	wanting very much *The child is eager to have the candy.* wanting to have or to do in a hurry *We were eager to get off the bus.*
matter	(mat′ ər)	be important *Nothing seems to matter when you are unhappy.* cause or reason for *Getting a new car was a matter of joy to me.* thing to do *This is a matter I must take care of.* makes a difference *Finishing school matters very much to me.*
pack	(pak)	fill with things; put things into *Take your books and pack them in this box.* a bundle of things wrapped up or tied together for carrying *We bought a pack of paper plates.* push closely together *Seven of us were packed into the car.* a number of the same kind of animals or men together *A pack of theives hit the town.*

My Man, Friday!

Special Words

Caribs	(kar′ ibs)	people of an Indian tribe in north eastern South America *Our class read about the Caribs in a history book.*
Christian	(kris′ chən)	one who believes in Christ and follows His teachings *Real Christians are kind, good, and happy people.*
master	(mas′ tər)	one who is in charge of someone or something *The dog's master feeds him and takes care of him.*
sword	(sôrd, sōrd)	a tool for fighting, usually metal, with a long sharp blade fixed in a handle *We watched two men fighting with swords in a show on television.*
tribe	(trīb)	a group of people joined by a common background and way of living *The cannibals live together as a tribe.*
Trinidad	(trin′ ə dad)	an island in the West Indies *The island of Trinidad is fairly large, and there are many people living there.*

Necessary Words

Friday	(frī′ dē, frī′ dā)	Robinson Crusoe's servant *Friday and Robinson Crusoe became good friends.*
grind	(grīnd)	crush into powder or small bits *A mill grinds wheat into flour.*
save	(sāv)	to keep from being hurt or from doing wrong *Many times, firemen save people from burning buildings.* keep aside, store up *I saved my money so that I could buy a car.*
spoke	(spōk)	to have said something *His friend spoke to him on the telephone.*
sweetest	(swēt′ est)	the kindest, nicest, best *My grandmother is the sweetest person I know.*
understand	(un′ dər stand′)	get the meaning of, know well *The student listened carefully to understand the question.*
war	(wôr)	a time of fighting *When a country is at war, many people are killed.*

My Man, Friday!

When Friday understood that he did not need to be afraid, he bowed down and set Robinson Crusoe's foot on his head. This was a sign that he would stay with Robinson Crusoe and do whatever he wanted in return for his life.

Preview:
1. Read the name of the story.
2. Look at the picture carefully.
3. Read the sentences under the picture.
4. Read the first two paragraphs of the story.
5. Then, answer the following question.

You learned from you preview that
____ a. Robinson Crusoe was dreaming.
____ b. cannibals were coming to the fortress.
____ c. cannibals were having a feast.
____ d. one man was trying to get away.

Turn to the Comprehension Check on page 52 for the right answer.

Now read the story

Read to find out how Robinson Crusoe and Friday got along together.

My Man, Friday!

One day, in 1684, an old dream began to come true. Five boats of cannibals were on the shore two miles from my fortress. I was watching through my telescope. They were cutting up one man for cooking when the next one broke away. He ran my way.

Three chased him. He crossed the little river and kept running. One couldn't swim; the others were much slower.

Quickly, I got two guns and ran out between the man and his chasers. I knocked out one and shot the other. The noise of my gun so frightened the man I was helping, that he was ready to fly away. But I called and made signs for him to come and not be afraid.

As he came, he spoke. I could not understand him. No matter! It was the sweetest sound in 25 years!

I smiled at him. He came close, put his head on the ground, and set my foot on his head.

Now, the cannibal I had knocked out, sat up. The man I was helping made signs asking for my sword. With one swish, he cut off the head of the cannibal — very cleanly. Then, he quickly made a big hole and packed sand over the two dead men.

At my cave, I gave him water, bread, and raisins. I made him understand that his name would be "Friday." It was on a Friday that I saved him. He would call me "Master." And I showed him the meaning of "Yes" and "No." We stayed in the cave that night.

Next morning, we went past the place where the two dead men were. Friday made signs that we should dig them up and eat them. But I showed such disgust that he left them alone.

The sight on the shore was terrible to me. Friday made nothing of it. I had him gather the pieces and burn them. He would have liked to eat some of the leftovers, but I let him know I would kill him if he did.

I took Friday to my fortress. There I gave him some pants from the shipwreck. I made a coat and some boots for him. One of the hats, I had already made, fit him. The boots and hat were more comfortable to him than the pants and coat. But he soon got used to wearing clothes.

I made a tent for him between my two fences. At night, I took my guns inside. I fixed the door so that it would make a loud noise if it were opened from the outside.

But I need not have been so careful. Friday was eager to please me. I cooked goat meat for him and he liked it. He signed to me that he would never eat man's flesh again.

Friday was eager to learn to do everything. I showed him how I ground the rice and barley into flour, made bread, and baked it. Very soon he did it as well as I. He learned to care for the goats. He picked grapes, dried them to raisins, and packed them in baskets for our food. By the end of the first year, Friday had already learned to talk in English pretty well. This was a matter of special joy to me.

Friday told me he had been on my island before. He showed me the place where he and his men had eaten people taken in war. It was on the other side of the island, where I had found the foot print.

Friday told me that the land I could see was the great island, Trinidad. Indian tribes lived on the main land and the islands nearby. They were all called Caribs.

Three years Friday and I lived together, alone. He showed himself to be good and true. I told him about God and read the Bible to him. He came to be a very good Christian. I learned to be a better one through teaching him. And we grew to love each other.

My Man, Friday!

COMPREHENSION CHECK

Preview answer:

d. one man was trying to get away.

Choose the best answer.

1. His old dream that came true was to
    _____ a. get a man away from the cannibals.
    _____ b. kill the cannibals.
    _____ c. keep the cannibals from having their feast.
    _____ d. chase the cannibals.

2. The man who was afraid of the noise of Robinson Crusoe's gun
    _____ a. chased the cannibals.
    _____ b. could not swim the river.
    _____ c. was the man he was helping.
    _____ d. made signs that he was not afraid.

3. He knew the man he was helping would not hurt him when
    _____ a. the man cut off the head of the cannibal.
    _____ b. the man set Robinson Crusoe's foot on his head.
    _____ c. the man packed sand over the two dead men.
    _____ d. the man knocked out the cannibals.

4. Friday would not dig up the cannibals to eat them because
    _____ a. Robinson Crusoe showed disgust.
    _____ b. Friday was not a cannibal.
    _____ c. Friday showed disgust.
    _____ d. Friday had bread and raisins to eat.

5. He was a little afraid of Friday at first because
    _____ a. Friday would not do as he asked.
    _____ b. Friday could not talk in English.
    _____ c. Friday was not a Christian.
    _____ d. he did not feel safe with a cannibal.

6. Friday's boots
    _____ a. were less comfortable than his pants.
    _____ b. came from the boat.
    _____ c. were made by Robinson Crusoe.
    _____ d. were terrible to him.

7. It was a special joy to Robinson Crusoe when Friday was able to
    _____ a. grind rice and barley into flour.
    _____ b. talk in English.
    _____ c. pack baskets with food.
    _____ d. care for the goats.

8. The land Robinson Crusoe had seen all these years was named
    _____ a. Brazil.
    _____ b. the great island.
    _____ c. Carib.
    _____ d. Trinidad.

9. Another name for this story could be
    _____ a. "I Talk to Cannibals."
    _____ b. "I Keep My Island Safe from Cannibals."
    _____ c. "Cannibals Try to Kill Me."
    _____ d. "I Save a Cannibal and Get a Friend."

10. This story is mainly about
    _____ a. fighting with cannibals.
    _____ b. finding and teaching Friday.
    _____ c. being afraid of cannibals.
    _____ d. getting Friday to wear clothes.

Check your answers with the key on page 67.

My Man, Friday!

VOCABULARY CHECK

cave	boots	eager	matter	pack	already

I. Sentences to Finish

Using the words in the big box above, choose the one which best fits in each of the sentences below. Write the words on the lines in the sentences.

1. Because we are going to the mountains, I will wear my _____ .

2. We all helped _____ our things into the car.

3. Everyone was _____ to get started.

4. In the mountains we stopped to visit a _____ .

5. I have _____ seen this cave.

6. Will it _____ if I don't go along?

II. Cross Word Puzzle

Fill in the little boxes with the letters of the words at the top of the page. The numbers in the puzzle match the numbers of the meanings below. The meanings will help you guess which word fits each set of boxes.

Across

4. Make a difference
5. Want very much
6. Put things into something

Down

1. Very tall shoes
2. Before now
3. A large hole in rocks

Check your answers with the key on page 71.

This page may be reproduced for classroom use.

We Win — and Get a Happy Surprise!

PREPARATION

Key Words

autumn	(ô′ təm)	the time of year after summer and before winter *In the <u>autumn</u> of the year, leaves fall from the trees.* fall season *The weather turns cool in the <u>autumn</u>.*
danger	(dān′ jər)	something that may hurt; chance of harm *A policeman's life is full of <u>danger</u>.* thing that may cause harm *Big rocks under water are a <u>danger</u> to ships.*
excitement	(ek sīt′ mənt)	something that excites; something that makes you happy or surprised *There was much <u>excitement</u> at our house when mother saw a mouse.* thing that stirs up feelings *The circus was an <u>excitement</u> in our town.* way of acting when stirred up *It was easy to see the <u>excitement</u> build up as our team pulled ahead.*
gun	(gun)	something used in hunting to kill animals *He fired the <u>gun</u> and killed the deer.* a long pipe made for shooting, mostly used for killing *People use <u>guns</u> in fighting and hunting.*
less	(les)	not so much *We have <u>less</u> rain here.* not so long *It was <u>less</u> than a week before I saw him again.* smaller amount or number *There are <u>less</u> than a hundred pennies in my bank.*
shot	(shot)	noise made when a gun is fired; used or fired a gun *The sound of a <u>shot</u> broke the morning quiet.* the act of shooting a gun; having pulled the trigger so that a ball of lead is fired from the gun *The hunter <u>shot</u> and killed a deer.*

We Win — and Get a Happy Surprise!

Special Words

chopped   (chopt)
cut into small pieces
We chopped potatoes to put in the soup.

pray   (prā)
to speak to God; to ask of God
You can pray to God at any time or any place.

puzzled   (puz' əld)
to have become mixed up and not able to understand something
The directions were so mixed up that we were puzzled about how to put the model airplane together.

rudder   (rud' ər)
a flat piece of wood or metal, joined to the end of a ship or boat; used to make it go in different directions
The sailor made the boat go around the island by turning the rudder.

Spaniard   (Span' yerd)
a person who lives or was born in Spain
My friend is a Spaniard, but she has been living in this country for many years.

yelling   (yel' ing)
crying out with a strong, loud sound
The two boys were fighting and yelling at each other.

Necessary Words

ax   (aks)
tool with a flat, sharp blade on a long wooden handle used for chopping or cutting wood
We have an ax to cut logs for our fireplace.

bloody   (blud' ē)
covered with blood
His pants got bloody from the cut on his leg.

clear   (klir)
when clouds do not hide the sun; bright, light
We waited for a sunny, clear day to take pictures.

clearly   (klēr' lē)
when something is said or done in a clear matter; plainly, understandably
The teacher explained the dance step very clearly.

mad   (mad)
to be very angry or upset
Mrs. Smith is mad at the dogs for digging in her garden.

mainland   (mān' land', mān' lənd)
the main part of a country or area of land; apart from its islands
We went from the island to the mainland by airplane.

tear   (tir)
when someone cries, the drops of water that come from the eyes
There were tears in her eyes after she read the sad story.

untie   (un tī')
undo; make free
Untie the dog and let him run.

We Win -- and Get a Happy Surprise!

When Robinson Crusoe and Friday went to get into the boat to chase the cannibals, they found a man. As Friday untied and helped him sit up, he was surprised and over joyed to see that the man was his own father!

Preview:
1. Read the name of the story.
2. Look at the picture carefully.
3. Read the sentences under the picture.
4. Read the first paragraph of the story.
5. Then, answer the following question.

You learned from your preview that Friday told Robinson Crusoe
_____ a.   there were many white men on the mainland.
_____ b.   he had never seen a white man before.
_____ c.   white men lived with his people "like brothers."
_____ d.   many white men would sail to his country.

Turn to the Comprehension Check on page 58 for the right answer.

Now read the story.

Read to find out how Friday came to find his father.

We Win — and Get a Happy Surprise!

I showed Friday the old long-boat that had washed to shore after our ship wreck. He looked at it carefully. "Me see such boat like this come to my land." A little less than four years ago, Friday told me, 17 white men came in the boat. They still lived with his people "like brothers."

One clear autumn day, from the top of a hill, we could see the mainland. Friday began dancing. "Oh, joy! Oh, glad! There see my country!"

I asked him, "Would you like to be back there?"

"Oh, yes!" he said, "If you go, too."

But I said, "Why, they would eat me!"

"No, no," said Friday. "I tell them. They much love you."

One day I told Friday we would make a big boat and he would go home in it. He looked very sad. "Why you angry mad with Friday? Why send Friday away?"

I asked, "Did you not say you wished to be there?"

"Yes, yes," said Friday, "wish we both there. No Master go; no Friday go!"

"But what would I do there?" I asked.

Very quickly Friday answered, "You teach wild mans to live new life. You tell them, 'Know God, pray God.' You tell them, 'Eat bread, milk, animals. But no eat man again'."

"Friday, I don't know enough to teach them. You go. I'll live by myself, as before."

Friday looked puzzled. He picked up an ax. "Take, kill Friday; no send Friday away!" There were tears in his eyes.

At that, I told him I would never send him away.

We set to work to make a boat big enough to go to the mainland. We found a big tall straight tree. We cut and chopped it into the shape of a boat. I made sails for the mast. Then I showed Friday how to work the sails and rudder. He was already very good at rowing.

That autumn we were busy putting things on board, getting ready for our trip. One morning Friday went to the shore to get turtle eggs. He came flying back. "Oh, Master! Oh, Master! Oh, BAD! Oh, BAD!"

"What's the matter, Friday?" I asked.

"Three boats. Many mans! Mans come for me!" he said in terrible excitement.

"We have our guns," I said. "Will you do what I say?"

Friday answered, "Me die when you say die, Master."

He was so frightened, that I gave him a drink of rum. I took one, too. Then we got the guns, swords, and an ax.

We went through the woods to a place where we could see clearly. The cannibals were already eating the first man. The next one was tied up on the shore. And he was not a cannibal; he had clothes on!

Just then, two cannibals went to get the next man. Friday and I shot our guns. We killed three men. We shot again. Five more fell. The others jumped around, bloody and yelling in great excitement. Friday and I ran out, shouting. Five cannibals jumped into a boat to get away from the danger. Friday shot and killed one.

I cut the ties on the man. "What are you?" I asked him.

"Christian," he answered.

When he spoke, I knew he was also a Spaniard. I gave him a drink of rum and some bread. Then, he was able to help us fight. He used a sword and a gun. Friday used the ax. In all, we killed 17 cannibals.

Four got away in the boats. We jumped into another boat to chase them. We thought there was a danger that they would come back with no less than 200 or 300 men.

In the boat, we were surprised to find another man tied up. I cut his ties. I had Friday give him some rum and tell him he was safe.

When the man sat up, Friday stopped and looked! Then he took him in his arms and cried for joy. The man was Friday's own father!

We Win -- and Get a Happy Surprise!

COMPREHENSION CHECK

Preview answer:

c.   white men lived with his people "like brothers."

Choose the best answer.

1. In autumn, they were able to clearly see
    _____ a.   the cannibals.
    _____ b.   Friday's country.
    _____ c.   an old longboat.
    _____ d.   white men.

2. Friday thought Robinson Crusoe was angry with him because
    _____ a.   Robinson Crusoe said they would build a boat and he would go home.
    _____ b.   Robinson Crusoe was afraid of cannibals.
    _____ c.   Robinson Crusoe did not want to see the 17 white men on the mainland.
    _____ d.   Robinson Crusoe did not want to go to sea again.

3. Friday wanted Robinson Crusoe to come to his country to
    _____ a.   teach his people.
    _____ b.   live by himself.
    _____ c.   eat bread and milk.
    _____ d.   learn to be a cannibal.

4. Robinson Crusoe did not have to teach Friday to row because
    _____ a.   they were going to sail, not row.
    _____ b.   he would not do the rowing.
    _____ c.   they were not building a rowboat.
    _____ d.   he already knew how to row.

5. They were going to win the fight with the cannibals by
    _____ a.   cutting off the cannibals' heads.
    _____ b.   using their guns to kill them.
    _____ c.   jumping in boats to get away.
    _____ d.   yelling in great excitement.

6. The first man they found tied up was
    _____ a.   a cannibal.
    _____ b.   a Carib.
    _____ c.   a Christian.
    _____ d.   Friday's "brother."

7. They did not want any of the cannibals to get away because
    _____ a.   the cannibals would bring many more back with them.
    _____ b.   the cannibals had Friday's father tied up.
    _____ c.   they thought the cannibals would take their boat.
    _____ d.   they thought it was right that cannibals should be shot.

8. The cannibals were going to
    _____ a.   bring his father to Friday.
    _____ b.   use his father to catch Friday.
    _____ c.   untie Friday's father and let him go.
    _____ d.   kill and eat Friday's father.

9. Another name for this story could be
    _____ a.   "A Trip to the Mainland."
    _____ b.   "We Build A Boat."
    _____ c.   "I Get Angry with Friday."
    _____ d.   "We Fight Cannibals."

10. This story is mainly about
    _____ a.   the cannibals killing and eating the Spaniard.
    _____ b.   building a boat and going to the mainland.
    _____ c.   Friday telling Robinson Crusoe he would never leave him.
    _____ d.   fighting with the cannibals and finding Friday's father.

Check your answers with the key on page 67.

We Win — and Get a Happy Surprise!

VOCABULARY CHECK

autumn	danger	excitement	less	shot	gun

I. Sentences to Finish

Using the words in the big box above, choose the one which best fits in each of the sentences below. Write the words on the lines in the sentences.

1. When the man wanted to kill the deer, he used a _____ .

2. The animals ran away when they heard a _____ .

3. You have more, but I have _____ .

4. He was afraid when his life was in _____ .

5. Leaves turn red and yellow in _____ .

6. My first trip on an airplane was filled with _____ .

II. Words in Sentences

Cross out the word that does not belong.

1. We didn't know there was (excitement, danger) all around us.

2. After the car wreck, there was great (excitement, danger).

3. Because we knew someone might get hurt, there was (excitement, danger) among us.

4. The falling roof of the burning building was a(n) (excitement, danger) to anyone standing on the sidewalk.

5. The (shot, gun) was heard across the fields.

6. The (shot, gun) made a loud noise.

Check your answers with the key on page 71.

This page may be reproduced for classroom use.

Back to England!

PREPARATION

Key Words

awake	(ə wāk′)	not asleep *She was awake very early in the morning.* come out of sleep *I like to hear the birds singing when I awake.*
forget	(fər get′)	not remember *Did I forget my book and leave it at school?* let go out of the mind; fail to remember *I must not forget all the rules of this game.* fail to think of; fail to do *Do not forget to go to the store on your way home.*
forgot	(fər got′)	not remembered *I forgot to bring my book home.* failed to remember *I forgot this was your birthday.* failed to think of; failed to do *I forgot one thing I meant to do today.*
lose	(lüz)	not able to find *If you lose your book, you will have to buy a new one.* not have any longer; have taken away by accident, parting, death, etc. *Robinson Crusoe did not lose his plantation by being away so long.* fail to keep *I do not want to lose what I have already won.*
promise	(prom′ is)	words said to say you will or won't do something *She made a promise to find the mittens.* to give one's word; to make a promise *The man promised to pay on the first day of every month.* words said or written to make sure someone will do or not do something *He made a promise to always be true to the teachings of his church.*
twenty	(twen′ te)	a number, two tens *She gave everyone twenty cents.* the number after 19 and before 21 *Count to twenty; make sure we have enough.*

Back to England!

Special Words

drunk	(drungk)	to have drank too much rum or other alcoholic drink *That man must be drunk; he is driving all over the road.*
fought	(fôt)	to have been in a fight *Many men fought in the war.*
Governor	(guv′ ər nər, guv′ nər)	one who is in charge of other people, and may be in charge of a town, a city, a state *Do you know the name of the Governor of your state?*
keepsake	(kēp′ sāk′)	something that is kept for a reason, usually to remember someone or something *I saved my school Year Book as a keepsake.*
nephew	(nef′ yü)	the son of one's brother or sister *My sister's boy, John, is my nephew.*
worst	(wėrst)	the least good; as bad as a thing can be *That shirt, with all the holes in it, is the worst piece of clothing he has.*

Necessary Words

December	(di sem′ bər)	the 12th and last month of the year *Christmas comes in December.*
hang	(hang)	put to death by hanging with a rope around the neck *The man was hanged at sun up.*
law	(lô)	a rule that must be followed by people living in a state or nation *It is against the law to drive a car through a red light.*
leader	(lē′ dər)	one who leads; the one who tells or shows the others what to do *The leader of our group walked in front as we made our way through the woods.*
married	(mar′ ēd)	when two people live together as husband and wife *My friend married a man from another town.*
order	(ôr′ dər)	a telling of what to do *The owner gave me orders to follow to get the job done.*
sailor	(sā′ lər)	a person whose work is handling a boat *The sailor spends most of his time out at sea.*
shooting	(shüt′ ing)	hitting or killing someone with a bullet from a gun *The boy likes shooting at the target.*
welcome	(wel′ kəm)	to receive gladly or kindly *We welcome our friends to our home.*
whole	(hōl)	all the parts of anything; complete *I gave my friend some of my books to read, but I kept the whole set as my own.*
women	(wim′ ən)	girls that are grown-up; they are not children *Women are usually smaller than men.*
yardarm	(yärd′ ärm′)	either end of a long pole used to hold up a square sail on a boat *The yardarm on the large sailboat is high up in the air.*

Back to England!

Wearing clothes given to them by the English Captain, Robinson Crusoe and Friday happily set sail for England. They took along the goat skin umbrella and cap, a parrot, and the box of money saved from the ship wreck more than 27 years before.

Preview:
1. Read the name of the story.
2. Look at the picture carefully.
3. Read the sentences under the picture.
4. Read the first paragraph of the story.
5. Then, answer the following question.

You learned from your preview that when the ship left for England, the one giving the orders was
_____ a. the Captain.
_____ b. Robinson Crusoe.
_____ c. the new "captain."
_____ d. Friday.

Turn to the Comprehension Check on page 64 for the right answer.

Now read the story.

Read to find out what happened to make Robinson Crusoe able to go back to England.

Back to England!

On December 19, 1686, I left for England. Here Friday and I were, on board an English ship. And the Captain and his men were all under my orders! How had that happened?

One day, Friday had thought he saw his father and the Spaniard coming back from the mainland. They had gone to get the 16 other Spaniards living with Friday's people.

But my telescope showed it was a longboat coming in from an English ship. That was strange!

We watched quietly. Three men sat down on the shore, looking very sad. The other eight got drunk and went to sleep out in the woods.

Friday and I crept down to the three. One was the Captain! The sailors had taken the ship away from him. As the eight woke up and came back, we tied them fast!

The twenty-six men still on the ship, fired guns for the boat to return. Finally, ten more men came to shore in another longboat. They spread out, looking for their lost mates. After dark, they came back to their boat, a few at a time. The Captain killed the leader. The others were tied up.

I kept out of sight. The Captain said "The Governor" had 50 men. Next morning, the Captain told them they must not forget what happens to men who take over ships. It was the law of England to hang them. Soon, every man was ready to help the Captain. They made a promise to keep him as a father as long as they lived.

That night the Captain took the 11 best men and boarded his ship. The new "captain" came out shooting. He was killed and hanged from the yard arm.

Next morning, I was not yet awake when the Captain came to my fortress, calling, "Governor! Governor!" He went on, "There's your ship. She is all yours, and so are we."

The Captain brought me a suit of his clothes. Now, I really looked like "The Governor."

We left the three worst men on the island. They wanted to stay. I showed them how to live comfortably. They promised to take care of things. I told them the Spaniards would come and to welcome them.

As keepsakes, I took my great goat-skin cap, my umbrella, and a parrot. I also took my money.

I came back to York, England, in the summer of 1687, after being away 35 years. By now, the only ones of my family still living were my two sisters and two sons of one brother.

My plantation in Brazil brought me a lot of money — much more than I had dreamed of. I found I did not lose any money from being gone so long.

Now, I did not forget all the people who had helped me. The Captain who took me to Brazil had kept books to keep track of the money from my plantation. The wife of the Captain from my first trading trip had kept money for me. I forgot that and gave her more.

I settled in York. I married and had three children. I gave money to my sisters. I helped my grown nephews. One went to sea. After five years, I put him in his own ship.

Then, my wife died in 1694. I found I could not forget my island. My nephew was going on another trading trip. I went with him.

We stayed on my island twenty days. The Spaniards had come and brought their women. There were twenty children. I gave parts of the island to the people to live on. But I kept the whole island as my own; I did not want to lose so much of my life's work. I sent English women, cows, sheep, and pigs to the people there.

Later, 300 Caribs came to take over the island. But the people fought them off. Ten years later, they were still living there. Even now, I still awake with happy dreams of my island.

Back to England!

COMPREHENSION CHECK

Choose the best answer.

1. The English ship stopped near the island
   _____ a. because they needed food and water.
   _____ b. to visit Robinson Crusoe and Friday.
   _____ c. to leave the Captain and his mates.
   _____ d. because the sailors had taken over the ship.

2. "The Governor" was
   _____ a. Robinson Crusoe.
   _____ b. Friday.
   _____ c. the Captain.
   _____ d. the first mate.

3. The Captain hanged the new "captain" from the yardarm because
   _____ a. he wanted to make Robinson Crusoe the captain.
   _____ b. it was the English law to hang him.
   _____ c. the new 'captain' had taken his ship.
   _____ d. he did not want his 11 men to board his ship.

4. The three worst men wanted to stay on the island because
   _____ a. they wanted to take care of it.
   _____ b. they wanted to welcome the Spaniards.
   _____ c. they would be hanged if they went back to England.
   _____ d. they would get lots of money if they stayed there.

5. Robinson Crusoe's keepsakes were
   _____ a. the English ship and Captain.
   _____ b. his suit of clothes and telescope.
   _____ c. his box of money from the shipwreck.
   _____ d. his goatskin cap and umbrella, and a parrot.

6. When he got to England, he found he had a lot of money
   _____ a. by being away 35 years.
   _____ b. in his box from the shipwreck.
   _____ c. from his plantation in Brazil.
   _____ d. from going on a trading ship.

7. He kept his island as his own because
   _____ a. he did not want to lose his life's work.
   _____ b. he did not want to give parts of it away.
   _____ c. he did not want the Spaniards to have it.
   _____ d. he wanted his nephew to have it.

8. Robinson Crusoe went back to the island at the end of the story because
   _____ a. he could not forget his life there.
   _____ b. he had promised Friday he would.
   _____ c. the Spaniards needed him as Governor.
   _____ d. 300 Caribs had come to take it over.

9. Another name for this story could be
   _____ a. "A Captain Gets His Ship Back."
   _____ b. "I Leave But Can Not Forget My Island."
   _____ c. "Caribs Come to the Island."
   _____ d. "I Get Married and Have Children."

10. This story is mainly about
   _____ a. what happened to Robinson Crusoe's family.
   _____ b. Spaniards on the island.
   _____ c. the English captain and his mates.
   _____ d. Robinson Crusoe getting off the island.

Check your answers with the key on page 67.

twenty

Back to England!

VOCABULARY CHECK

awake	forget	forgot	lose	promise	twenty

I.   Sentences to Finish

Using the words in the big box above, choose the one which best fits in each of the sentences below. Write the words on the lines in the sentences.

1.   Yesterday was such a beautiful day that I _____ about my work and went on a picnic.

2.   I do not want to _____ to buy bread on my way home.

3.   You never really _____ by being kind.

4.   To _____ feeling happy is a great way to start a day.

5.   I made $10 for one job and $10 for the next; then I had _____ dollars.

6.   If you do this, I _____ you will not be sorry.

II.   Words of Same Meaning

From the box above, choose the word which means the same as the one(s) underlined in each sentence. Write the one you choose on the line after the sentence.

1.   There were <u>ten and ten</u> of us playing the game. _____

2.   I can <u>not have any longer</u> this old thing and never miss it. _____

3.   When my clock rings in the morning, I <u>come out of sleep</u> with a start. _____

4.   I <u>failed to remember</u> to go by the store to buy milk. _____

5.   I will <u>fail to remember</u> the things I don't like, and think about the things I do. _____

6.   I <u>give my word</u> that I will always remember you for this kind thing. _____

Check your answers with the key on page 72.

NOTES

COMPREHENSION CHECK ANSWER KEY
Lessons CTR C-1 to CTR C-10

LESSON NUMBER	QUESTION NUMBER										PAGE NUMBER
	1	2	3	4	5	6	7	8	9	10	
CTR C- 1	(d)	d	(d)	a	d	(b)	c	(a)	△d	□b	10
CTR C- 2	c	b	(b)	(d)	a	(c)	a	d	△c	□b	16
CTR C- 3	c	b	d	b	a	(c)	d	(c)	△a	□d	22
CTR C- 4	b	a	(c)	c	a	d	b	(a)	△d	□d	28
CTR C- 5	c	(a)	d	(d)	(c)	a	b	d	△c	□c	34
CTR C- 6	a	b	a	b	c	a	(b)	(d)	△d	□a	40
CTR C- 7	d	d	(c)	b	(a)	b	(b)	d	△b	□a	46
CTR C- 8	(a)	c	(b)	a	(d)	c	b	d	△d	□b	52
CTR C- 9	b	a	a	(d)	b	c	a	(d)	△d	□d	58
CTR C-10	(d)	(a)	(c)	(c)	d	c	a	(a)	△b	□d	64

○ = Inference

△ = Another name for the story

□ = Main idea of the story

VOCABULARY CHECK ANSWER KEY
Lessons CTR C-1 to CTR C-10

1   I LONG FOR THE SEA   11

I.
1. bundle
2. bend
3. gather
4. roots
5. son
6. snapped

II.

```
              ¹B E N D
              U
              N
     ²S       D
      N       L
    ³G A T H E ⁴R
      P       O
      P     ⁵S O N
      E       T
      D       S
```

2   EIGHT YEARS LATER — AND SHIP WRECKED   17

I.
1. chatter
2. blanket
3. freeze
4. curtain
5. enjoy
6. crept

II.

```
                    ¹F
                    R
                    E
      ²C H A T T E R
      U             E
      R             Z
      T             E
    ³B L A N K E T
      I
    ⁴E N J O Y
```

3   SETTLING IN   23

I.
1. thirty
2. class
3. hang
4. crack
5. finally
6. replied

II.
1. class
2. hang
3. thirty
4. crack
5. replied
6. finally

VOCABULARY CHECK ANSWER KEY
Lessons CTR C-1 to CTR C-10

4 I FIND PEACE — AND GROW TO BE HAPPY   29

I.
1. special
2. jar
3. desk
4. job
5. hall
6. sidewalk

II.
sidewalk — place between rooms
hall — place to walk at the side of the street
desk — glass with a wide mouth to store things in
jar — not like others
job — special table to write on
special — work that someone has to do

(matching lines indicate:)
- sidewalk → place to walk at the side of the street
- hall → place between rooms
- desk → special table to write on
- jar → glass with a wide mouth to store things in
- job → work that someone has to do
- special → not like others

5 I TRULY WORK FOR MY BREAD   35

I.
1. worry
2. coach
3. team
4. bench
5. chance
6. lose

II.
1. (team, ~~coach~~)
2. (~~worry,~~ chance)
3. (~~lose,~~ worry)
4. (coach, ~~team~~)
5. (bench, ~~coach~~)
6. (~~team,~~ lose)

6 QUIET HAPPENINGS — AND FRIGHTENING!   41

I.
1. chew
2. meat
3. spoil
4. meant
5. dash
6. rid

II.

```
          ¹D
  ²M E A T       ³R
  E     ⁴S P O I L
  A       H     D
  N
  T
```

VOCABULARY CHECK ANSWER KEY
Lessons CTR C-1 to CTR C-10

LESSON NUMBER		PAGE NUMBER

7   CANNIBALS ON MY ISLAND!   **47**

I. 1. rule
2. moment
3. fur
4. rush
5. sidewalk
6. mile

II. fur — animal skins
mile — measure used to tell how far it is from one town to another
moment — a very short time
rule — things to do and not do
rush — hurry
sidewalk — place to walk beside a street

8   MY MAN, FRIDAY!   **53**

I. 1. boots
2. pack
3. eager
4. cave
5. already
6. matter

II.

Crossword:
1. BOOTS (down)
2. ALREADY (down)
3. COVES (down)
4. MATTER (across)
5. EAGER (across)
6. PACK (across)

9   WE WIN — AND GET A HAPPY SURPRISE!   **59**

I. 1. gun
2. shot
3. less
4. danger
5. autumn
6. excitement

II. 1. (excitement, danger)
2. (excitement, danger)
3. (excitement, danger)
4. (excitement, danger)
5. (shot, gun)
6. (shot, gun)

VOCABULARY CHECK ANSWER KEY
Lessons CTR C-1 to CTR C-10

I.
1. forgot
2. forget
3. lose
4. awake
5. twenty
6. promise

II.
1. twenty
2. lose
3. awake
4. forgot
5. forget
6. promise